# American History Stories...
## *...you never read in school*
## *...but should have.*

*Volume I: The Shot Heard 'Round the World*

### REPRINTED FROM THE ORIGINAL SCHOOL TEXTBOOK OF 1889

By Mara L. Pratt, M.D.
with an Introduction by
Reed R. Simonsen

D0030083

*EIGHTH PRINTING*

On the Cover: "The Prayer at Valley Forge."
  © 1992 Arnold Friberg R. S. A. This painting is used
by permission of Friberg Fine Art Prints. Those wishing
to acquire a print may write: Valley Forge Prints, 1220
Valley Forge Road—P.O. Box 987/0088, Valley Forge,
PA 19482 or call: 1-800-4VF-1776.

I.S.B.N. 0-9640546-0-4

*PRINTED IN THE UNITED STATES OF AMERICA*

# Introduction to New Edition

by Reed R. Simonsen

It was a cold and rainy day in September when I stepped from my car to the pavement. The rain drizzled miserably in a way found only in the Mid-West. I had been drawn to a handmade sign which read: "CHURCH BOOK SALE, COME IN AND SUPPORT US!"

Book sales have always been a weakness of mine and it seemed to me as though the car voluntarily found its own parking place.

I climbed the wooden steps and pushed open a creaky door. The oldest woman in the world sat perched precariously on a stool, reading a book.

"Magazines are a dollar," she said without looking up, "and all books are as marked."

The smell of old leather filled the room, there were books everywhere. I was sure that I had died and come to some strange book-lovers heaven. The wisdom of hundreds of years lay stacked on plywood shelves, under tables and piled in rows along the floor. Truly pitiful is the man that cannot read the magic of Tennyson, the emotion of Jefferson or the splendor of Shakespeare. I thumbed through countless volumes, wishing for an extra life-time to read each book.

Near the front of the door was a small sign that read, "Rare Books." I made my way to the shelf and glanced at the titles. Pushed between two large books was one entitled simply: <u>American History Stories</u>. I chuckled under my breath, American History wasn't rare. I had many books on American History. I pulled the book from the shelf.

The front cover was worn colorless and the pages groaned with age. Printed on the inside flap was: School District #48.

An occasional blot of ink, as from a quill pen, spattered the pages and everywhere were signs of antiquity. Damaged pages were lovingly repaired to guarantee extended service. I paid the woman two dollars and fifty cents for it.

For many days it sat on my desk, old and retired from duty. On a sleepless night, I lifted it carefully from its place. Perhaps it still had one student left to instruct. As I began to read the beautiful histories, tears filled my eyes. I had studied history from elementary school to the university but I had never read stories such as these.

The morning sun found me finishing the last chapter. For the first time in my life I understood the glory that was America. I understood the dream, I never really did before. I had, for just a moment, come in touch with my heritage, my people, my country.

I wanted to meet the author of this book. I wanted to thank her. Thank her for loving this land as much as I did and for recording that love in print so that another generation could feel it.

I have shared these stories with others since. Their response has always been, "Why haven't I heard these stories before?" This is why I reprinted this book.

America is a land like no other. The ideas that drove the founders to build her are as visionary today as they were so many years ago, maybe more so. The men, women and children that sacrificed everything for future generations were noble, god-fearing and selfless people.

As Americans, we come from a proud heritage, a people that believed in freedom, self responsibility and happiness. Their ideas were worth fighting for, even dying for. They still are.

May the shot heard 'round the world, fired so long ago, echo in your heart today and always.

## About the Cover

In 1975, Arnold Friberg created his most famous masterpiece, "The Prayer at Valley Forge." As an artist, Mr. Friberg has earned his place as one of the great modern masters. He has painted hundreds of portraits and has received many distinguished awards. Arnold Friberg drew his first picture of George Washington at age twelve. Through the years, his respect and admiration for the great patriot grew, culminating in the depiction of General Washington praying for his country amid the trials of Valley Forge. It pays tribute to the man who led our struggling nation to victory, a man that believed in our nations motto: "In God We Trust."

# CONTENTS.

# CONTENTS.

PATRICK HENRY DELIVERING HIS CELEBRATED SPEECH, 1765.

# AMERICAN HISTORY STORIES.

## CAUSES OF THE REVOLUTION.

YOU remember, in the French and Indian War, the colonists began to feel dissatisfied with the way England treated them. Up to that time, England had left them pretty much alone; but as soon as she found they were really beginning to be quite important, that they were carrying on quite a little commerce and manufacturing, that they were raising quite a large amount of cotton and tobacco, and were really growing every year in wealth, and in numbers, and in power, then she thought it quite time that they be made to help support the English government.

The colonists, since they still considered England their mother country, were quite willing to do this, and would have done it had England treated them fairly.

Did you ever think where the money comes from to keep

in order the cities or town you live in — to build its public buildings, to lay out its streets, and to pay all the officers and workmen for their work?

Of course you know that every State has a Governor, who has been chosen by the votes of the people. He stands as the head man in the State; but of course he could not go about to every house to ask the people what they would like to have done in their particular cities or towns.

And so the work is divided; somewhat as the school system is in large towns and cities. There is a Superintendent, who has the charge of the teaching in the town or city; but as he could not teach ever child, he engages a principal to take charge of each school building, and each principal, in his turn, has a teacher to take charge of each room in the building.

The government of the State is somewhat like this — in its division at least. All the men of one town go to the "polls," as they call it, and vote for some one man to represent them. They tell him what they want, and he is expected, when he meets at the State House with the representatives from all the other parts of the State, to express the wishes of these men who have voted to have him fill this office.

The State calls these representatives together, finds what each town wants, and the money which all these property owners in all the towns have paid in, is distributed as these representatives think best.

In the same way, the work is divided in each city or town. The men all go to the polls again for a *municipal election*, as it is called; that is, to elect men to carry on the city affairs. They elect one man to oversee the whole city, much as the Governor oversees the whole State, and as the Superintendent oversees the whole school system. Then there is another man elected to oversee the water supply, another to oversee the roads, another to collect the taxes — and many, many more; so many that, rather than take time here to try to name them, I think I will leave you to ask your fathers about them; for very likely they can explain it all to you a great deal better than I can on paper.

But all these officers must be paid for working for the city, and the must also have money to carry on the work that is expected of them. And this money is raised by taxation, — that is, every property holder pays in a certain amount of money to help pay the expenses of the town or city. The tax-payers are willing to do this, because they know it will all go to pay the salaries of these officers, to build the roads, lay out public parks, support the schools, — all those things that go to help make our cities and towns pleasant and comfortable.

This sort of tax paying is perfectly just; because each town in this way gets its share of the good things which its tax money has bought.

Now let us see what England tried to do, — what it was

that made the colonies so angry that at last they rose in arms against the mother country.

She said, " You are getting so wealthy now, you ought to pay a tax to us."

The colonists said, "Very well, we shall be glad to do so ; for we consider ourselves as little towns belonging to England, and so of course we expect to give our share of the money which the government needs."

"But you are not to have any of this money back again," said England. "The king will do what he pleases with it. Neither are you to send any representative to us, and we will hear none of your prayers."

Then the colonists were angry indeed. "We are not slaves," said they, "and we are not going to pay money to England unless we can have representatives and be treated like the towns in England."

But greedy England only laughed at them, and said, "You shall do as we tell you to, or we will send our soldiers over to whip you into obedience."

England didn't realize that the colonies might perhaps be able to whip the British soldiers themselves.

Now I hope from all this, — and this has been a pretty long lesson I fear, — I hope you will understand, and will never forget, that the reason the colonists made war with England was because England was determined to tax them without allowing them any part in the government. As the histories say, the cause of the Revolution was

*" Taxation without Representation."*

## THE STAMP ACT.

One of the first things England did to raise money from the colonists, was to issue the *Stamp Act*.

The king sent over a large amount of paper on which had been put a certain *stamp*. This paper the king ordered the colonists to use in all their government writing.

Nothing, so the king said, would be considered of any value unless it was written on this stamped paper. For example, suppose a man owed another man a hundred dollars. When he paid the debt, the receipt would not be considered of any value unless it was

written on this particular paper. Suppose a young man and maiden were to go before the minister to be married; the marriage was not legal, so the king said, unless the minister did the writing, which was always given the married bride and groom, on this stamped paper.

Now, as the king had put a very high price upon this paper, you can see how, by compelling the American colonists to buy it, it was but one way of getting a heavy tax from them.

---

## BEHAVIOR OF THE COLONISTS.

The colonists all over the contry were furious when this stamped paper was sent to them.

The Boston people declared they wouldn't buy one sheet of it ; they would buy nothing, sell nothing ; the young men and maidens would not get married ; they would do nothing, indeed, which should compel them to use this stamped paper.   To show their contempt for the whole matter, they made a straw figure of the English officer who had the paper to sell, dressed it in some old clothes of his, and hung it on a big tree on Boston Common.

In New Hampshire, the people paraded the streets with a coffin on which was written, " Liberty is dead." They carried it to the grave, had a "make-believe" funeral and then, just as they were about to bury it, some one shouted, "Libery is not dead ! "

Then they drew up the coffin and carried it through the

streets again; crying, "Liberty's alive again! Liberty's alive again!"

In Charleston, South Carolina, stood an old tree, known as "Liberty Tree." It was a great live oak, growing in the centre of the square between Charlotte and Boundary Streets.

During the excitement over the Stamp Act, about twenty men, belonging to the "best families" in the state, assembled beneath this tree to hear an address by General Gadsen.

With vigor he condemned the measure, and urged his hearers to resist to the utmost such abominable tyranny.

This is said to have been the first public address of the kind that had been delivered in the colonies.

The men, after hearty cheers, joined hands around the tree, and pledged themselves to "resist English oppression to the death."

The names of these men are still on record. Most of them were indeed true to their pledge and, distinguished themselves in the war that followed, by their courage and patriotism.

This "Liberty Tree" was regarded with such reverence by the patriotic Carolina people, that Sir Henry Clinton, who held Carolina after its surrender to the British, ordered it to be destroyed. It was cut down, and afterwards its

branches were heaped about the trunk and the whole burned.
A mean act, one would say, to burn an unoffending tree;
but perhaps Sir Henry had in mind the old anecdote
which, if I remember rightly, runs something like this:

"Why do you kill me, an innocent trumpeter? I have
not fought against you."

"Very true," replied the captor; you may not fight yourself, but you incite others to fight. Hence I kill you."

In Pennsylvania, William Bradford, the editor of the
*Pennsylvania Journal*, came out with a "final issue," at the
head of which were "skulls and crossbones," pickaxes and
spades, all suggestive of the death-blow that had been
struck at the press. This number of the journal was deeply
embellished with heavy black margins, and was in truth a
most dolorous looking affair, as you may see from the picture on the next page.

In Virginia, a young man, named Patrick Henry, so
stirred up the people that the old men, angry as they were
with England, were frightened, and begged him to be
careful what he said.

Benjamin Franklin was sent to England by the colonists
to see what could be done. When he reached there, he
found that many of England's greatest men were on the
side of the colonists.

One of the men in the English government rose and
made a speech against the colonists, in which he said,

The TIMES are Dreadful. Dismal. Doleful. Dolorous. and DOLLAR-LESS.

# THE PENNSYLVANIA JOURNAL;

## AND WEEKLY ADVERTISER.

Thursday, October 31. 1765.

NUMB 1195

### EXPIRING: In Hopes of a Resurrection to LIFE again.

I AM sorry to be obliged to acquaint my Readers, that as The Stamp Act, is fear'd to be obligatory upon us after the first of November ensuing, (the fatal To-morrow) the Publisher of this Paper unable to bear the Burthen, has thought it expedient to stop a while, in order to deliberate, whether any Methods can be found to elude the Chains forged for us, and escape the insupportable Slavery, which it is hoped, from the last Representations now made against that Act, may be effected. Mean while, I must earnestly Request every Individual of my Subscribers, many of whom have been long behind Hand, that they would immediately Discharge their respective Arrears, that I may be able, not only to support myself during the Interval, but be better prepared to proceed again with this Paper, whenever an opening for that Purpose appears, which I hope will be

WILLIAM BRADFORD.

An Emblem of the Effects of the STAMP. O! the fatal Stamp.

Adieu Adieu to the LIBERTY of the PRESS.

" What ! will these Americans, these children of ours, who have been planted by our care, nourished by us, protected by us, will they now grudge us their money to help throw off our heavy debt ! "

Up jumped Colonel Barre. "Planted by your care, indeed ! It was your persecution that drove them to America in the first place ! " he cried.

"Nourished by you ! When have you nourished them? They have grown up by your very neglect of them ! Protected by you ! Have they not just now been fighting with your soldiers to protect *you*, rather, from the French and Indians ? "

And good William Pitt of England ! He arose and made a speech which, by and by, every boy and girl should learn. He said, " We are told that the Americans are obstinate ; that they are in almost open rebellion against us. I *rejoice* that America *has* resisted. I rejoice that they are not so dead to all feelings of liberty as to be willing to submit like slaves ! "

Hurrah for William Pitt and Colonel Barre ! Don't forget, all you little American men and women, that we had good friends in England then as we have now. There were lovers of liberty in that country, who were as eager as we were to resist all unjust laws.

## DAUGHTERS OF LIBERTY.

People who write histories always tell how brave and bold and patriotic the men and boys are; but very seldom do they think it worth while to tell of the brave deeds of the women and girls. Now, I don't think this is fair at all, do you girls? And you, little boys, if your sisters had done something just as brave as your brothers had done, wouldn't you be very indignant if every body should come to your house and praise your brothers, and cheer them, and all the time shouldn't speak one word to your sisters?

I am sure you would; manly, brave hearted boys are always ready to stand up for their sisters, and are always very angry when some one hurts or neglects them in any way.

Now, of course the mothers and maidens couldn't take guns and swords and go into battle as the men did, although they did even do that in some cases. But let us see what they did do. Somebody must stay at home and take care of the children, and the homes, and keep up the farms. So the brave women said to their husbands and sons, "You go into the battle-field, because you are stronger and larger and know about war; we will stay at home and keep the children cared for, that they may grow up strong to help you by and by; we will spin and weave day and night to keep you in yarn for stockings, and in cloth for clothes and blankets to keep you warm; we will plant, and harvest, and grind the corn, and do all your work on the farm that there may be food to send you, and food to keep you from starving when you all come home again."

What, think you, would the brave men in any war do if it were not for the brave women back of them at home to keep them from starving? O, it is a mean, cowardly man who would say that because the women didn't go forth in battle array that they didn't do their half in saving our country from the British soldiers!

Let us see who these "Daughters of Liberty," as they called themselves, were.

As soon as the trouble between England and America broke out, the men had formed themselves into societies, and had called themselves "Sons of Liberty." They pledged themselves to do everything in their power to drive back the English rule. The women, too, not wishing to appear to be one step behind their fathers, and husbands, and brothers, formed themselves into societies—"The Daughters of Liberty." They pledged themselves not to buy a dress, or a ribbon, or a glove, or any article whatever that came from

England. They formed spinning societies to make their own yarn and linen, and they wove the cloth for their own dresses and for the clothes of their fathers and brothers, and husbands and sons.

"The Weaving Room"

The women used to meet together to see who would spin the fastest. One afternoon a party of young girls met at the house of the minister for a spinning match. When they left, they presented the minister with thirty skeins of yarn, the fruit of their afternoon's work. The old women, some of whom were too old to do very much work, pledged themselves to give up their tea-drinking because the tea came to them from England, and because England had put a heavy tax on it. These dear old ladies, who loved their tea-drinking so much, bravely stood by their pledge. They drank catnip, and sage, and all sorts of herb teas, and pretended they liked it very much; but I suspect many an old lady went to bed tired and nervous, and arose in the morning with an aching head, all for the want of a good cup of tea.

At that time, there appeared in the newspapers many verses written by the English officers, no doubt, often making fun of these brave women, old and young. Here is one of the verses:

> " O Boston wives and maids, draw near and see,
> Our delicate Souchong and Hyson tea;
> Buy it, my charming girls, fair, black or brown,
> If not, we'll cut your throats and burn your town."

" Within eighteen months," wrote a gentleman at Newport, R. I., " four hundred and eighty-seven yards of cloth and thirty-six pairs of stockings have been spun and knit in the family of James Nixon of this town." In Newport and Boston the ladies, at their tea-drinkings, used, instead of imported tea, the dried leaves of the raspberry. They called this substitute Hyperion. The class of 1770, at Cambridge, took their diplomas in homespun suits, that they too might show their defiance of English taxation without representation.

## THE BOSTON BOYS.

Here is a story about the Boston boys, which is a match for the one you have just read about the Boston girls.

On Boston Common the boys used to skate and coast and build forts, just as other boys do to-day. Perhaps their skates weren't quite so elegant as those the Boston boys have now, and very likely their sleds were clumsy, home-made affairs, not at all like the beautiful double-runners and the toboggans you boys are so proud of; nevertheless those little lads then had just as jolly times, coasting down the same hills and skating on the same ponds.

The English had, by this time, become so convinced that the colonists were preparing for war, that they sent over a large detachment of red-coated soldiers. These soldiers made their headquarters in Boston, and soon became generally disagreeable to the people.

The boys had been watching eagerly the freezing of the ice on the pond on the common.

"To-morrow," thought they, "the ice will be strong enough to bear; and then, hurrah for the skating!"

Eagerly the boys hastened to the pond in the morning, their skates over their shoulders, their faces bright with the thought of the pleasure before them; but what do you suppose the cowardly soldiers had done during the night? Having nothing else to do, they had broken the ice all over the pond — and just to bother these little boys. Don't you think those great, strong soldiers must have had very mean hearts to go to work to plague little boys in that manner?

I am inclined to think these boys were pretty angry when they learned who had done this cowardly act, and very likely they scolded furiously about it.

Again and again the soldiers did the same thing. At last, one day when the boys were building a fort, some of these soldiers came idling along and knocked down the fort with their guns.

The boys, now angry through and through, determined no longer to bear this mean treatment.

"Let us go to General Gage," said one of the boys, "and tell him how the soldiers are treating us; and if he is any kind of a man, he will put a stop to it."

And go they did at once. With eyes ablaze with anger, they marched into the presence of the great English general.

After they had laid their wrongs before him, he said, "Have your fathers been teaching you, too, to rebel, and did they send you here to show their teachings?"

"Nobody sent us, sir," answered the leader; "but your soldiers have insulted us, thrown down our forts, broken the ice on our pond, spoiled our coasts, and we will not stand it."

General Gage could not help laughing at the earnestness of these plucky little fellows. He promised that the soldiers should not bother them any more ; then turning to

GENERAL GAGE.

an officer near by, he said, "Even the children here draw in the love of liberty with the very air they breathe."

## A BRAVE LITTLE GIRL.

While General Gage held the town of Boston, our people

were nearly starved, because of the number of British soldiers that must be fed. Accordingly, men were sent into the surrounding villages to obtain help. "Parson White," of the little town of Windham, urged his people to give all they could; and his little daughter, catching the spirit of loyalty, wondered how *she* could help the suffering Bostonians. Soon after, the villagers prepared to send Frederic Manning to the town with sheep and cattle and a load of wheat. The little girl thought of her pet lamb. *Could* she, *ought* she to part with it? Running to her father, she eagerly asked his advice; but the parson, smiling kindly, said, "No, dear; it is not necessary that your little heart be tried by this bitter strife;" and bade her run away and be happy. But the thought would not leave her. There in Boston were little girls, no older that herself, crying for food and clothing; she *must* give all she could to help

them. At last the day came on which the cattle and supplies of help were to be driven to town. Choking down her
sobs, the little martyr untied her pet from the old apple-
tree, and, crossing the fields, waited for Manning, the
driver, at the cross-roads.

"Please, sir," said she, her lip quivering, and the tears
rolling down her cheeks, "I want to do something for the
poor starving people in Boston — I want to do my part, but
I have nothing but this one little lamb. Please, sir, take it
to Boston with you, but, couldn't you carry it in your arms
a part of the way — 'cause it — it — it is so little, sir?"
Then bursting into tears and throwing her apron over her
eyes as if to shut out the sight of her dear little pet, she
ran away towards her home. Poor, brave little girl! I
hope when she told her mamma and papa what she had done,
that they took their little girl up in their arms and kissed
her many, many times, and told her what a dear, brave
little girl she had been. I suspect the tears were in their
eyes, too, when she told them; and I have always wished
the good parson had sent a fleet messenger to overtake the
driver and bring back the little lamb to its loving owner;
for I think it took more real courage to give up that one
pet lamb, than it did for the Boston boys to go before
General Gage when the soldiers had spoiled their fort.

TABLET ON THE CRISPUS ATTUCK'S MONUMENT, BOSTON

# THE BOSTON MASSACRE.

Soldiers who would be mean enough to bother little boys as these soldiers had done, would be pretty sure to get into trouble with the citizens by their mean acts.

They had entered the town, one quiet Sabbath morning, but instead of coming in quietly and doing whatever it was necessary to do in a quiet way, they came in with colors flying, and drums beating, as if, for all the world, they had conquered the city. Then, as if this were not insult enough, they took possession of the State House, and then marched to the Common, where they set up their tents, planted their cannon, and indicated to the enraged citizens, in every way, that they were going to stay.

Frequent quarrels took place between these soldiers and the people. One day they fell into an "out-and-out" fight.

Nathaniel Hawthorne, an author who has written such beautiful stories for you children,— The Snow Image ; The Wonderful Book ; Grandfather's Chair, etc.,— gives the following account of the Boston Massacre :

It was now the 3d of March, 1770. The sunset music of the British regiments was heard as usual throughout the town. The shrill fife and rattling drum awoke the echoes in King street, while the last ray of sunshine was lingering on the cupola of the town-house. And now all the sentinels were posted. One of them marched up and down before

the custom-house, treading a short path  through the snow,
and longing for the  time when  he would  be  dismissed to
the warm fireside of the guard-room.

In the  course of  the  evening  there  were  two  or three
slight commotions, which  seemed to  indicate that  trouble
was at hand.   Small parties of young men stood at the cor-
ners of the street, or  walked  along the  narrow pavements.
Squads of  soldiers, who  were dismissed  from duty, passed
by them, shoulder to shoulder, with the regular  step which
they had learned at the drill.   Whenever  these encounters
took  place,  it  appeared  to  be  the  object  of  the  young
men  to  treat the soldiers  with as much  incivility  as possible.

"Turn out, you lobster-backs ! " one would say.   " Crowd
them off the  side-walks ! " another  would cry.   " A  red-
coat has  no  right  in Boston streets."     " Oh,  you  rebel
rascals ! " perhaps the soldiers  would reply, glaring fiercely
at the young men.  " Some day or  other  we'll  make  our
way through Boston streets at the point of the bayonet ! "

Once or twice such disputes as these brought on a scuffle ;
which passed off, however, without attracting much  notice.
About eight  o'clock, for some  unknown  cause, an alarm-
bell rang loudly and hurriedly.   At the sound many people
ran out of their houses, supposing it to be an  alarm of fire.
But  there were no  flames to be  seen, nor was  there  any
smell of smoke in the clear, frosty air ;  so that most of the

townsmen went back to their own firesides.   Others, who were younger and less prudent, remained in the streets.

Later in the evening, not far from nine o'clock, several young men passed down King street, toward the custom-house.   When they drew near the sentinel, he halted on his post, and took his musket from his shoulder, ready to present the bayonet at their breasts.   "Who goes there?" he cried in the gruff tone of a soldier's challenge.   The young men, being Boston boys, felt as if they had a right to walk in their own streets without being accountable to a British red-coat.   They made some rude answer to the sentinel.   There was a dispute, or perhaps a scuffle.   Other soldiers heard the noise, and ran hastily from the barracks to assist their comrade.

At the same time many of the townspeople rushed into King street by various avenues, and gathered in a crowd about the custom-house.   It seemed wonderful how such a multitude had started up all of a sudden.   The wrongs and insults which the people had been suffering for many months now kindled them into a rage.   They threw snow-balls and lumps of ice at the soldiers.   As the tumult grew louder, it reached the ears of Captain Preston, the officer of the day.   He immediately ordered eight soldiers of the main guard to take their muskets and follow him.   They marched across the street, forcing their way roughly through the crowd, and pricking the townspeople with their bayonets.

A gentleman (it was Henry Knox, afterwards general of the American Artillery) caught Captain Preston's arm. "For heaven's sake, sir," exclaimed he, "take heed what you do, or there will be bloodshed!" "Stand aside!" answered Captain Preston, haughtily; "do not interfere, sir. Leave me to manage the affair." Arriving at the sentinel's post, Captain Preston drew up his men in a semi-circle, with their faces to the crowd. When the people saw the officer, and beheld the threatening attitude with which the soldiers fronted them, their rage became almost uncontrollable.

"Fire, you lobster-backs!" bellowed some. "You dare not fire, you cowardly red-coats," cried others. "Rush upon them," shouted many voices. "Drive the rascals to their barracks! Down with them! Down with them!"

"Let them fire if they dare!" Amid the uproar, the soldiers stood glaring at the people with the fierceness of men whose trade was to shed blood,

Oh, what a crisis had now arrived! Up to this very moment the angry feelings between England and America might have been pacified. England had but to stretch out the hand of reconciliation, and acknowledge that she had hitherto mistaken her rights, but would do so no more. Then the ancient bonds of brotherhood would again have been knit together as firmly as in old times. But, should the king's soldiers shed one drop of American blood, then it was a quarrel to the death.    Never, never would America rest satisfied, until she had torn down royal authority, and trampled it in the dust.

"Fire, if you dare, villains!" hoarsely shouted the people, while the muzzles of the muskets were turned upon them; "you dare not fire!"    They appeared ready to rush upon the levelled bayonets.    Captain Preston waved his sword, and uttered a command which could not be distinctly heard amid the uproar of shouts that issued from a hundred throats.    But his soldiers deemed that he had spoken the fatal mandate, "Fire!"    The flash of their muskets lighted up the street, and the report rang loudly between the edifices.

A gush of smoke overspread the scene.    It rose heavily, as if it were loath to reveal the dreadful spectacle beneath it.    Eleven of the sons of New England lay stretched upon the street.    Some, sorely wounded, were struggling to rise again.    Others stirred not, nor groaned, for they were past all pain.    Blood was streaming upon the snow; and that purple stain, in the midst of King Street, though it melted away in the next day's sun, was never forgotten nor forgiven by the people.

At once the bells were rung, and the citizens, rushing out to learn the cause, hastened to the fight.    The people in the country around, hearing the bells, hurried in with their muskets to help the town.    At last the soldiers, seeing that the whole country around was aroused and rushing to the rescue, took to flight.

HOUSE IN DANVERS WHERE THE " BOSTON TEA PARTY " PLOT IS SAID TO HAVE
BEEN TALKED OVER

# THE BOSTON TEA-PARTY.

This Boston tea-party was a very different sort of a party from the quiet little tea-parties to which your mammas like to go. There were no invitations sent out for this tea-party, and the people who attended it behaved in a very queer way, considering they were at a tea-party.

This was the way it came about. The English had put a tax, you will remember, upon nearly everything, tea included.

Now, when they found that the colonists were so furious about it, and seemed so determined to stand up for their rights, the English began to be afraid, and to think that perhaps they had gone a little too far.

So, wishing to soothe the angry colonists, they took off the tax on everything *except* the tea. "We will keep the tax on that," said the English, "just to let the colonists know that we have the *power* to tax them, and that they must obey; but we will not ask them to give us their money on the other things."

Foolish people, to suppose the colonists were going to be quieted in that way. It wasn't the money that they were made to pay that had angered them; they were willing to pay that; but it was the *idea* of their being taxed *without* representation !

"Does England suppose it is the few paltry dollars that we care for?" said they. "No; we will show her that, while we would be willing to pay thousands of dollars if we were treated fairly, we will not pay *one cent* when she treats us like slaves ! "

Not many days had passed before word came that a great vessel was nearing the harbor, loaded with tea.

A lively meeting was held in Faneuil Hall, and afterwards in the Old South Church ; and the people all declared that the tea should never be allowed to be brought ashore.

At evening the vessel was seen slowly nearing the wharf. Everything was quiet, and you would never have imagined what was going to happen.

Slowly the ship comes in, nearer and nearer the little wharf. Now, with a heavy swash of water and a boom, she touches ; out jump her sailors to fasten her ropes.

But hark ! what noise is that? It is the Indian war-whoop. And see ! down rush the Indians themselves, yelling and brandishing their tomahawks. In an instant they have boarded the vessel. Down into the hold they go, yelling and whooping at every step.

The terrified sailors stand back aghast. Out they come again, lugging with them their heavy chests of tea.

Still they yell and whoop ; and over go the chests into the dark water below.

And now, when every chest is gone, suddenly the Indians grow very quiet ; they come off from the deck ; and, orderly, take their stand upon the wharf; then do we see that they were not Indians at all.    They were only men of Boston disguised.

This then was the Boston tea-party, which took place in Boston Harbor on the evening of December 16, 1773.

Three hundred and forty-two chests were thrown overboard.

On their way home the party passed the house at which Admiral Montague was spending the evening.    The officer raised the window and cried out, " Well, boys, you've had a fine night for your Indian caper.    But, mind, you've got to pay the fiddler yet."    "Oh, never mind," replied one of the leaders, " never mind, squire ! Just come out here, if you please, and we'll settle the bill in two minutes."    The admiral thought it best to let the bill stand, and quickly shut the window.

The Americans had taken one great step towards liberty, and the English had been taught a lesson of American grit.    It would have been well for England had she been wise enough to heed it.

THROWING THE TEA OVERBOARD.

Words by SEBA SMITH.

1. There was an old La - dy, lived o - ver the sea, And
2. "Now Moth - er, dear Moth - er, the daugh-ter re - plied, "I

she was an Is - land Queen; . . Her daughter liv'd off in a
sha'n't do the thing you ax, . . . I'm will-ing to pay a fair

new countrie, With an o-cean of wa - ter be - tween; . .
price for the tea, But nev - er the three-pen-ny tax;" . . .

The old lady's pockets were full of gold, But nev-er content-ed was
"You shall," quoth the mother, and reddened with rage, For you're my own daugh-ter, you

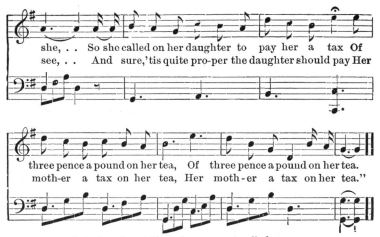

she, . . So she called on her daughter to pay her a tax Of
see, . . And sure,'tis quite pro-per the daughter should pay Her

three pence a pound on her tea, Of three pence a pound on her tea.
moth-er a tax on her tea, Her moth-er a tax on her tea."

3 And so the old lady her servant called up,
  And packed off a budget of tea,
And eager for three pence a pound, she put in
  Enough for a large familie,
She ordered her servants to bring home the tax,
  Declaring her child should obey,
Or old as she was and almost woman grown,
  She'd half whip her life away,
  She'd half whip her life away.

4 The tea was conveyed to the daughter's door,
  All down by the ocean's side,
And the bouncing girl pour'd out every pound
  In the dark and boiling tide;
And then she called out to the Island Queen,
  "O Mother, dear Mother," quoth she,
"Your tea you may have when 'tis steeped enough,
  But never a tax from me,
  No! never a tax from me."

## THE PATRIOTIC BARBER.

**There** were some of the colonists who did not approve of this rebellion of the people against the king. Although they knew England had no right to do what she had done, still they dreaded a quarrel; and, since they were pretty comfortable, didn't care much whether England treated them as equals or as slaves. There were some, too, who had such great reverence for England and the king, that they would have considered it an honor to have their ears pulled or their faces slapped, if only it were done by a king's hand.

These colonists who believed in obeying the king, no matter what he demanded, were called Tories, while those colonists who were so ready to fight for freedom were called Whigs.

I am afraid a great many of the Tories were persecuted in those days by the excited Whigs.

There is a story told of a Boston barber, which will show you how bitterly the Whigs hated the Tories.

A barber was shaving a customer one day, and, at the same time, earnestly talking politics with him. One side of the customer's face was nicely shaved, when, by something he said, the barber learned that the man was a Tory.

Quick as a flash the barber threw down his razor, clutched the man by the collar and dragged him to the door.

"A Tory! a Tory!" shouted the barber at the top of his voice. In less than a minute a crowd had gathered. A roar of laughter went up at sight of the unhappy Tory, his eyes glaring with rage and fright, his face all lathered, one side cleanly shaven, the other all rough with his bristling beard.

STREET SCENES.

Away ran the man, and after him ran the crowd, hooting and laughing, and shouting "A Tory! a Tory!" The crowd followed him from shop to shop, until at last he found a barber who was himself a Tory, and who willingly rescued him from the mob and finished the shaving for the unfortunate man. This was a very mean act in the Whig barber, but, it will show you very well the spirit of the times.

# BATTLE OF LEXINGTON.

In the spring of 1775, General Gage was told that the Americans had for a long time been secretly carrying to some place outside of Boston stores of gunpowder, guns, muskets and bullets, that there might be a supply whenever they were needed. He also learned that, in every town and village about Boston, companies were being formed for military drill. These men called themselves "Minute-men," because, as they said, they would be ready to enter battle against the British any time at a minute's notice.

Gage began to watch these signs of fight on the part of the colonists. Into all the towns about he sent spies to learn all they could about these military stores and these minute-men. Soon he learned that it was in the old town of Concord that the colonists were storing their ammunition.

"We will start out some dark night and capture those stores" said Gage.

"We will watch the British soldiers," said the Americans, "and see that they do not start off in the night to capture our stores."

"The colonists will be asleep," said General Gage,

STATUE TO THE CONCORD MINUTE MEN

"and, if we are quiet, they will know nothing of our departure."

"We will keep our eyes on you, General Gage," said the colonists, "night and day ; for we suspect you would like to steal our ammunition."

But as General Gage did not hear the colonists say these words, and had not yet learned that the colonists were fully as sharp as his own soldiers, he knew not that sentinels were pacing back and forth all night long, watching him ; and that messengers were standing ready with their strong horses to ride out into the outlying towns with the alarm, if the British troops were seen to show any signs of marching.

At last, on the evening of April 18, 1775, one of these sentinels heard sounds and saw a stirring among these soldiers. Soon he saw them creep quietly down to the water and hurry into boats. There was no doubt now that the British were planning to cross the Charles River and set out for Concord.

In twenty minutes, two mounted horsemen were galloping away to rouse the farmers in all the towns around and warn them to be up and ready for fight. One of these messengers was Paul Revere ; and as our own poet Longfellow has told the story of his ride in a way that all readers, little ones and big ones, like to hear, I think that instead of trying to tell it to you myself, I better write you the story of "Paul Revere's Ride" just as Longfellow himself told it.

PAUL REVERE'S RIDE.

# PAUL REVERE'S RIDE.

Listen, my children, and you shall hear
Of the midnight ride of Paul Revere.
On the eighteenth of April in 'Seventy-five;
Hardly a man is now alive
Who remembers that famous day and year.

He said to his friend, "If the British march
By land or sea from the town to-night,
Hang a lantern aloft in the belfry arch
Of the North Church tower as a signal light,—
One if by land, and two if by sea,
And I on the opposite shore will be,
Ready to ride and spread the alarm
Through every Middlesex village and farm,
For the country-folk to be up and to arm."

Then he said "Good-night!" and with muffled oar
Silently rowed to the Charlestown shore,
Just as the moon rose over the bay,
Where swinging wide at her moorings lay
The Somerset, British man-of-war;
A phantom ship, with each mast and spar
Across the moon like a prison bar,
And a huge black hulk that was magnified
By its own reflection in the tide.

Meanwhile, his friend, through alley and street,
Wanders and watches with eager ears,
Till in the silence around him he hears
The muster of men at the barrack door,
The sound of arms, and the tramp of feet,

And the measured tread of the grenadiers
Marching down to their boats on the shore.

Then he climbed to the tower of the Church,
Up the wooden stairs with stealthy tread,
To the belfry chamber overhead,
And startled the pigeons from their perch,
On the sombre rafters, that round him made
Masses and moving shapes of shade,—
Up the light ladder, slender and tall,
To the highest window in the wall,
Where he paused to listen and look down
A moment on the roofs of the town,
And the moonlight flowing over all.

  .  .  .  .  .  .  .

Meanwhile, impatient to mount and ride,
Booted and spurred, with a heavy stride
On the opposite shore walked Paul Revere.
Now he patted his horse's side,
Now gazed at the landscape far and near,
Then, impetuous, stamped the earth,
And turned and tightened his saddle girth;
But mostly he watched with eager search
The belfry-tower of the Old North Church,
As it rose above the graves on the hill,
Lonely and spectral and sombre and still.

And lo! as he looks, on the belfry's height
A glimmer, and then a gleam of light!
He springs to the saddle, the bridle he turns,
But lingers and gazes, till full on his sight
A *second* lamp in the belfry burns!

A hurry of hoofs in a village street,
A shape in the moonlight, a bulk in the dark,
And beneath from the pebbles, in passing, a spark
Struck out by a steed that flies fearless and fleet:
That was all! And yet, through the gloom and the light,
The fate of a nation was riding that night;

  .    .    .    .    .    .    .    .    .

It was twelve by the village clock
When he crossed the bridge into Medford town.
He heard the crowing of the cock,
And the barking of the farmer's dog,
And felt the damp of the river fog,
That rises after the sun goes down.

It was one by the village clock,
When he rode into Lexington.
He saw the gilded weathercock
Swim in the moonlight as he passed,
And the meeting-house windows, blank and bare,
Gaze at him with a spectral glare,
As if they already stood aghast
At the bloody work they would look upon.

It was two by the village clock,
When he came to the bridge in Concord town.
He heard the bleating of the flock,
And the twitter of birds among the trees,
And felt the breath of the morning breeze
Blowing over the meadows brown.

  .    .    .    .    .    .    .    .    .

So through the night rode Paul Revere;
And so through the night went his cry of alarm
To every Middlesex village and farm, —
A cry of defiance and not of fear,

A voice in the darkness, a knock at the door,
And a word that shall echo forevermore!
For, borne on the night-wind of the Past,
Through all our history, to the last,
In the hour of darkness and peril and need,
The people will waken and listen to hear
The hurrying hoof-beats of that steed,
And the midnight message of Paul Revere.

---

In the little town of Lexington, a hundred brave minute-men awaited the coming of the British army. Of course there was no hope that a hundred farmer-soldiers could drive back the large army, but they were ready to do what they could.

Up came the red-coats with Major Pitcairn at their head. "Disperse, ye rebels," cried the major; "disperse! throw down your arms and disperse!" But the brave minute-men stood their ground. They neither threw down their arms nor did they disperse. Then one of the British officers, angry that they should dare defy him, discharged his pistol into the little band.

Now the minute-men, who had been told not to fire until they were fired upon, promptly returned fire, wounding three of the British soldiers. This was answered by a fierce volley from the British, and when the army passed on, they left eight brave farmer-soldiers dead upon the green.

Then, on the troops marched straight to Concord, their band playing Yankee Doodle — a song which had been composed by them to deride the colonists.

"Play Yankee Doodle, you old lobster backs," cried some boys from behind a fence; "but look out, Lord Percy, that you don't play "Chevy Chase" when you come back."

Now, as it happens that "Chevy Chase," was an old song of a battle in which this very Lord Percy's ancestors had figured, and had been defeated, you can imagine the young officer didn't enjoy the boy's joke very well; especially when some of his fellow-officers, who could appreciate a good joke even if they couldn't appreciate the courage of the colonists, joined in the laugh against him.

On reaching Concord, the troops took possession of the ammunition, rolled a hundred barrels of flour into the river, and started on, intending to cross the bridge at Concord. But there they found the brave minute-men mustered on the bridge, a hundred and fifty strong.

CONCORD BRIDGE—THE SCENE OF THE FIGHT.

Immediately the command to fire was given, and two of the minute-men fell dead. Now there blazed back a volley from the little band, which compelled the British troops to fall back. From that moment the colonists had the best of the British troops.

Another volley, and away went the red-coats in full retreat back towards Lexington, the minute-men in full pursuit. On, on, the red-coats ran, while from every house and barn, from behind every fence and bush, rang the quick snap of muskets, shooting down the red-coats at every step. On, on, they ran, panting for breath (their tongues, so an English historian says, hanging out of their mouths), until they came into Lexington again.

Here they were met by Lord Percy's troops. These troops formed a hollow square about them; and they, breathless and exhausted, sank upon the ground, too breathless even to tell what had happened. Lord Percy's troops thus closed about them, and led them, when they had gained strength enough to march again, back to Boston. But all the way they were pursued and shot at on all sides by the colonists concealed by the roadside, until they were glad indeed, at sunset, to get back under the protection of the guns of the British man-of-war.

# THE ORIGIN OF YANKEE DOODLE.

Words by GEORGE P. MORRIS.

1. Once on a time old John-ny Bull Flew in a rag-ing
2. Then down he sate in bur - ly state, And bluster'd like a
3. John sent the tea from o'er the sea With heav-y du-ties

fu - ry, And said that Jon - a - than should have No
gran-dee, And in de - ris - ion made a tune Call'd
rat - ed; But wheth - er hy - son or bo - hea, I

tri - als, sir, by ju - ry: That no e - lec-tions
"Yan - kee doo - dle dan - dy." "Yan - kee doo - dle"—
nev - er heard it stat - ed. Then Jon - a - than to

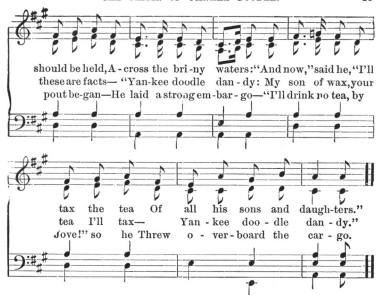

should be held, A - cross the bri -ny waters:"And now,"said he,"I'll
these are facts— "Yan-kee doodle dan - dy: My son of wax,your
pout be-gan—He laid a strong em-bar - go—"I'll drink no tea, by

tax the tea Of all his sons and daugh-ters."
tea I'll tax— Yan - kee doo - dle dan - dy."
Jove!" so he Threw o - ver - board the car - go.

4 Then Johnny sent a regiment,
  Big words and looks to bandy,
Whose martial band, when near the land,
  Play'd "Yankee doodle dandy,"
"Yankee doodle—keep it up!
  "Yankee doodle dandy!
"I'll poison with a tax your cup,
  "Yankee doodle dandy."

5 A long war then they had; in which
  John was at last defeated—
And "Yankee doodle" was the march
  To which his troops retreated.
Cute Jonathan to see them fly,
  Could not restrain his laughter:
"That tune," said he, "suits to a T,
  I'll sing it ever after."

6 With "Hail Columbia!" it is sung,
  In chorus full and hearty—
On land and main we breathe the strain,
  John made for his tea-party.
"Yankee doodle—ho!—ha!—he!
  "Yankee doodle dandy—
"We kept the tune, but not the tea,
  "Yankee doodle dandy!"

7 No matter how we rhyme the words,
  The music speaks them handy,
And where's the fair can't sing the air
  Of "Yankee doodle dandy!"
"Yankee doodle—firm and true—
  "Yankee doodle dandy,
"Yankee doodle, doodle doo!
  "Yankee doodle dandy."

## THE WOMEN AT LEXINGTON.

But what do you suppose the women of Lexington and Concord were doing all this time? They were not idle, you may be sure. Every bit of pewter that could be found, old pewter tea-pots, and sugar-bowls, pewter spoons — many of which were old heirlooms, and were therefore very dear to these women's hearts — all were melted and made into shot. Their very dresses they tore into pieces to furnish wadding for the muskets; and on all sides might the women have been seen loading and reloading the muskets that drove back the British troops.

One woman, Dame Batherick, had taken her musket and gone down into the field to work. Being a "lone" woman, she had heard nothing of the morning fray, and had as usual gone out to work upon her farm.

As the British came fleeing back from Concord, Dame Batherick heard the guns and whistling balls. Pausing in her work and screening her eyes from the sun, she eagerly gazed across the fields towards the village. Nearer and nearer came the sound of battle; she saw the village blaze; she heard the shouts of the soldiers.

"'Tis war," she cried; "war, and blood, and fire!"

Seizing her musket she started forward. Just then a squad of red-coats broke through the bush full upon her sight. In an instant her quick woman's wit took in the whole situation.    Drawing herself proudly up, her eyes flashing fire, she cried, "Halt! as ye value life, advance ye not another step."

" Ye are my prisoners, sirs!    March on! " she said;
    Then dropped her plants and pointing out to them the way,
She drove them quickly on, as she had oft ahead
    Driven the kine across the fields, at set of day;
And they, "King George's own," without a word obeyed.

Over the fields so green she marched her captive band,
    Her dark eyes flashing still, her proud heart beating high
At thought of England's outrage on her native land!
    For women were true patriots in the days gone by,
And scorned the foreign yoke, the proud oppressor's hand.

And thus this rustic dame her captives safe did bring
    Unto a neighbor's house; and, speaking fearless then,
In words whose every tone with woman's scorn did ring,
    She said unto King George's brave and stalwart men
" Go, tell the story of your capture to your King!

" He cannot crush our rights beneath his royal hand
    With dastards such as you!    And ere this war be done
We'll teach old England's boasting red-coat band,
    We're not a race of slaves!    From mother, sire, to son,
There's not a coward breathes in all our native land! "

Thus Mother Batherick's fearless deed was done;
    Long will the tale be told in famed historic page,
How, in this first great victory by freemen won,
    A dame with furrowed brow and tresses white with age,
Captured the grenadiers at famous Lexington.

RUINS OF TICONDEROGA.

## CAPTURE OF TICONDEROGA.

After this battle of Lexington, a Continental Congress met in Philadelphia to talk over this battle and to decide what was to be done. War must follow—of this they all felt sure. And so troops must be raised, a leader appointed, and some plan of action be agreed upon. It was at this time that George Washington was appointed " Commander-in-chief of all the forces raised or to be raised in defence of American liberties."

The news of the battle had been carried throughout the colonies, and in every town the women were knitting and spinning clothes for their husbands and brothers and sons, and making all preparation for war; the men were drilling and forming themselves into companies, ready to march to Boston at the first word of command.

In Vermont, called in your geographies, you remember, the "Green Mountain State," the men had formed themselves into a company under their colonel, Ethan Allen, and called themselves the "Green Mountain Boys." On the morning of the very day of the meeting of this Congress which had made Washington Commander-in-chief, Ethan Allen, with a detachment of these volunteers, set out to surprise Fort Ticonderoga. Arriving there in the early gray of the morning, he found all but the sentries sound asleep. Suddenly, that no time might be given for an alarm, Allen's band rushed into the fort, and, making their way directly to the sleeping apartments of the commander, Allen, in a voice like thunder,— so his followers say,— demanded the instant surrender of the fort.

The commander, frightened, and only half dressed, threw open his door, saying, "By whose authority do you —" But Allen broke in upon him with, "In the name of the Great Jehovah and the Continental Congress do I command you to surrender." No resistance was attempted; and so a large quantity of cannon and ammunition which the English had stored there, and which just then was so much needed by the troops at Boston, fell into the hands of the Americans, without the loss of a single man.

## BATTLE OF BUNKER HILL.

Great indeed was the excitement throughout the colonies when the news of the battle of Lexington was carried from town to town. Meetings were called in every town, congresses were held, armies formed — for everyone knew now that war had indeed begun. Soon, some fifteen thousand men collected from the different colonies about Boston, and these succeeded in giving General Gage a good scare.

All this time the king of England and his counsellors were fretting and fuming because of the obstinacy of the American colonists. They sent over more troops, and when General Gage heard of their arrival he began to grow brave again. He sent out a proclamation, saying that if the colonists would lay down their guns and say they were sorry, he would see that the government of England forgave them and received them into English favor again — all but Samuel Adams and John Hancock; those two men, he said, were past forgiveness, and ought rather to be hanged. It is needless to say that the colonists were not at all moved by General Gage's generous offer of forgiveness. They kept straight on about their plans.

On the 16th of June, a detachment of the American soldiers, outside of Boston, was commanded to go over to Charlestown and fortify Bunker Hill.

Under the cover of darkness, the soldiers climbed Breed's

Hill, this being nearer Boston, and quietly threw up the earth in such a way as to form ditches and forts. Imagine the surprise of the British the next morning, when they looked across the water and found the Americans working away, busy as bees, finishing up their night's work.

The British cannon were turned upon them, but in vain. "We must march up the hill ourselves," said General Howe; and soon three thousand soldiers were on the way to attack the Americans. Eagerly the soldiers watched from behind their embankment; eagerly the British troops in Boston watched; and eagerly watched the women and children from the house-tops. O it was a terrible day for dear old Boston!

Up the hill climbed the British soldiers, firing at every step. At the top, behind the embankment, crouched the brave fifteen hundred, silent as death.

"Boys," said good Colonel Prescott, "we have no powder to waste; aim low; and don't fire until you can see the whites of their eyes."

And so, I suppose, the British, receiving no shots as they climbed the hill, thought they were going to climb straight over the entrenchments into the American quarters. But, as we know, these Americans had other plans.

The red-coats were nearly up the hill. Their waving plumes were nearly on a level with the hill-top. "Fire," commanded the officer. Bang! bang! bang! bang! went

BATTLE OF BUNKER HILL.

the fifteen hundred muskets. The British soldiers fell, mowed down like grain before the scythe. Then on they came again. Again, bang! bang! bang! went the fifteen hundred muskets; and again the British fell back in dismay. It was a long time before they made their third attack; and the hearts of the brave men within the intrenchment, and the brave women praying from the house-tops, beat high in the hope that the battle was over.

But soon the British forces rallied, and made one mighty rush over the dead bodies of their fallen brothers, upon the intrenchment. The Americans were now, many of them, without powder; and although they battled hand to hand with clubs and stones, the British reached the summit, and drove the Americans down the hill to Charlestown Neck.

Bunker Hill.     Charlestown.     Breed's Hill.

This was the first regular battle of the Revolution; and although the Americans were defeated, still the defeat brought about so many good results, that, after all, perhaps it was quite as good as a victory; for it showed the British soldiers and the British king that the colonists were not to be subdued by simple threats; while, on the other hand it fired the colonists with courage and zeal. They know now that there was no escape from war; they had learned that, untrained though they were, they could fight even the British regulars; they knew that, had their ammunition not given out, the day would have been theirs. And so, although they had lost some of their bravest men and although they had been defeated, there was no feeling of discouragement in the hearts of the colonists.

---

# GENERAL WARREN.

We must not leave the story of the Battle of Bunker Hill without speaking of the brave General Warren. He was indeed one of the bravest of the brave. He was a man of wonderful talent, and from the very earliest troubles with England had been one of the staunchest patriots. When he learned that the British were setting out to attack the colonists on Breed's Hill, he started out at once across Charlestown Neck, amid showers of British balls; and, on reaching the redoubt, offered himself as a volunteer.

The poet makes him say to the colonists as the British draw near:

> " Stand! the ground's your own my braves!
>   Will ye give it up to slaves?

Will ye look for greener graves?
  Hope ye mercy still?
What's the mercy despots feel?
Hear it in that battle-peal!
Read it on yon bristling steel!
  Ask it — ye who will.

" In the God of battles trust!
Die we may — and die we must;
But, oh, where can dust to dust
  Be consigned so well,
As where heaven its dews shall shed,
On the martyred patriot's bed,
And the rocks shall raise their head.
  Of his deeds to tell? "

Throughout the battle, Warren was in the thickest of the fight; and at the end, when the British had gained the redoubt, he was one of the last to give up the struggle. He was rallying the few remaining colonists, when a British officer who knew him, and knew what a power he was among his countrymen, singled him out and shot him.

When General Gage heard that Warren was dead, he said, " It is well; that one man was equal to five hundred ordinary soldiers."

He had been an honorable citizen, a skilled physician, a noble senator, and a brave warrior. The loss of no one man, in the whole war was mourned more, perhaps, than the loss of this hero, General Warren.

## THE MARCH TO QUEBEC.

In 1775, the Americans began looking longingly towards Canada. Ever since the success at Ticonderoga, Ethan Allen and Benedict Arnold had been saying, "Send us to Montreal and Quebec! Let us take them as we took Crown Point and Ticonderoga!"

Washington knew what a grand thing it would be for the American army to get possession of these cities; but he also knew something which very few beside himself knew; and that was, that the American army had not enough powder to carry on their work, where they were, much longer unless help came. For this reason he held back some time. Many officers and soldiers heaped abuse upon Washington's head for this, and nearly accused him of being cowardly.

He endured their blame however, for he dared not let it be known how low the powder supply was growing.

Finally, in the early fall two armies were ordered into Canada. One under General Mongomery, the other under Benedict Arnold. General Montgomery led his division up through New York and down the St. Lawrence to Montreal, while Benedict Arnold led his division up through Maine.

Montgomery's soldiers were a wretched looking set — ragged and dirty, shoeless and hatless,— but still willing to march on and fight for their loved country. On reaching Montreal they found that the British soldiers had been all called into the colonies, and that the city was therefore without defence. Of course the city was taken with little or no trouble, and in the army marched. It is a terrible thing to ransack a city as this army ransacked Montreal, but as long as wars go on these things must be done; and since it has to be done here, we cannot but be glad that it was our own brave men who fell upon the riches of this city. Such treasures as they did find! not so much money, but food and clothing! Blankets and warm shirts, jackets and trousers, stockings and shoes!

They thought it almost worth while to have marched all this distance just to be once more warmed and clothed and fed. They remembered, too, the other soldiers who were coming up through Maine, and would soon be with them, and they carried off enough of all these good things for them, as well.

Montgomery, leaving a part of his soldiers to hold Montreal, now marched on to Quebec, where Arnold was to join forces with him.

When Arnold came, he had a terrible story to tell. Their march up through Maine had been almost as terrible as the " Winter at Valley Forge," of which you will read later on. The army had come up the Kennebec River in boats, and when they had come to places where they could not push along their boats, they had carried them on their backs until open places again were found.

It had been so bitterly cold ! they had marched waist deep through icy water, and had lain down in their wet clothing night after night in the freezing forests. Their clothes ragged enough when they set out, could now hardly be kept together; their shoes, in this five-hundred-mile march, had been worn to nothing, and many a soldier had frozen his feet. Their provisions, too, had given out, and many of the soldiers had eaten the leather of their shoes and knapsacks, so hungry were they.

Many of these poor men, overcome by starvation and sickness, had turned back discouraged. Some of them afterwards succeeded in getting back to Massachusetts, but more died lost in the forests.

Arnold had with him a brave young man named Aaron Burr, who acted the part of a hero in this terrible march, and in the attack that followed. When Montreal was

reached, Burr started on another hundred miles to tell
Montgomery that Arnold's forces were ready to join him in
the attack on Quebec.

It was now December — the last day of the year.   A
severe snowstorm was raging — a real blizzard, we should
call it now — and in the very midst of it, the command came
for the attack upon Quebec.

QUEBEC.

Now there were very few soldiers in the city, and it
would have been a very easy thing to take this city — as
easy as it had been to take Montreal — only that this city
was a " walled city," and more than that, it was situated

high up on bluffs or cliffs overlooking the river. You can see how hard it was for the army outside to get up to this city, and how easy it was for the army within the city to sweep them down with their fire.

A terrible, almost hand to hand battle followed. One battery had been taken by the Americans, and they were just attacking the second.

"Follow me, my brave boys," called Montgomery, "and Quebec is ours!"— but just then, down came a volley of grape shot from the garrison above, striking dead this brave leader and mowing down the soldiers on every side of him. Dismayed at the loss of their leader, the men in the rear turned and fled — and Quebec was lost to our side.

When young Aaron Burr, who was standing beside Montgomery in the foremost ranks. saw his leader wounded, he caught up the falling body, and, staggering under the load, dragged it down the bluffs beyond the reach of the fire of the enemy.

Arnold remained for some time in Canada, hoping to find a chance to attack the city again; but the soldiers in the city were on the watch, and before very long British soldiers arrived to help them; then there seemed nothing for him to do but to march home with the broken army, and so leave Canada to the British.

## WASHINGTON AND HIS ARMY.

Now that the war had really begun, events followed upon each other thick and fast. Before the summer was over, every colony, from New Hampshire to Georgia, was up in arms.

Washington had gathered his army outside of Boston, and there he held General Gage imprisoned in the city. Washington had now several good generals to help him, one of whom, called " Old Put," was famed far and wide for his pluck. In another chapter you will read about Old Put's wolf hunt — a story you must know; for although it is not exactly a story of the Revolution, still it does no harm to know any story of the heroes of the Revolution that tells of the daring courage of these men.

But we were speaking of Washington's army. In a " History of Our Country," written by Abby Sage Richardson, is the following excellent description of the appearance of the Colonial army.

"You can form no idea what a task lay before Washington and his generals. Here was a great body of men hurried into the field from farms and workshops, with no more idea of military drill than a herd of sheep, with miserable old muskets, scanty supply of powder and balls, and no money to buy any. Then the dress of this provincial army was enough to excite the laugh which the British soldiers raised at them.   Some of them were dressed in the long-tailed linsey-woolsey coats, and linsey-woolsey breeches, which had been spun and woven in farm-house kitchens; some wore smock frocks like a butcher, also made of homespun; some wore suits of British broadcloth, so long used for Sunday clothes that they had grown rather the worse for wear; and every variety of dress and fashion figured in these motley ranks.

"When General Washington rode grandly out on horseback, dressed in his fine blue broadcloth coat, with buff

BRITISH SOLDIERS.

colored facings, buff waistcoat and breeches, a hat with black cockade, and a sword in an elegantly embroidered sword-belt, I think his heart must have sunk within him as he looked on his tatterdemalion army, and then glanced over towards Boston, and thought of the British soldiers, gorgeous in their elegant new uniforms, trained to march up to the cannon's mouth like a solid wall in motion."

But for all that Washington knew that his army was brave, and in dead earnest, for were they not fighting for their own homes, their own mothers and wives and children?

Two brothers in Washington's army, to show what skilful marksmen they were, took a board only five inches wide and seven inches long, fastened a piece of white paper the size of a dollar upon it in the middle, and then shot at it at a distance of sixty yards.

Eight bullets they fired; and everyone of them went straight through the white paper. When the lookers on wondered at them, they said, "There are fifty more men in our company who can do just as well." They then offered to shoot apples off each other's heads, as William Tell is said to have done long, long ago; but their commander said they had shown their comrades that they could, beyond a doubt, send a bullet straight through the heart of a British soldier, and that now they had better save their powder till a British soldier appeared.

And so you see, that, although these men were so oddly dressed, and although they knew so little of military training, yet they had clear heads and straight eyes, and, above all, dauntless courage.

## The Red-coats Leave Boston.

All this time, you remember, Washington's army had kept the British imprisoned in the city. They had been unable to get out into the country for provisions, and now they were in real danger of starvation. They were short of fuel too. They had already chopped down several wooden houses, and had even been mean enough to chop down the "Old North Church" for firewood. These cowardly soldiers knew that these simple-hearted Puritans loved their meeting-houses as they loved their homes; and so they took great delight in showing all the contempt they could for these places. They liked nothing better than to break the glass and shoot into the windows as they passed along. The old South Church, which the Boston children know, and which still stands on Wash-

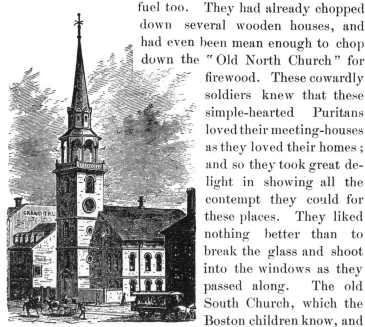

OLD SOUTH CHURCH.

ington Street, was turned into a riding school. The pews

were torn out, and the floor strewed with litter for the horses. One of the pews in this church, a very beautifully carved pew, they carried away to build a fence for a pig-pen. I could not begin to tell you of the needlessly cruel and insulting things these red-coats did to annoy the people of Boston.

Faneuil Hall, now called " the cradle of Liberty," because throughout the history of Boston, so many liberty meetings of all sorts have been held there, was made into a theatre : and there the British army used to delight to meet and listen to plays and songs which were sure to be full of jokes on the American colonists.

At one time the British were acting a play which they had named the " Blockade of Boston." In this play was an actor intended to represent George Washington. He was dressed in some ridiculous manner, wore a funny looking wig, and carried a rusty old sword.

Just as this character was coming upon the stage, another clownish looking figure with another big rusty sword by his side, an officer rushed upon the stage crying, "The Yankees are attacking our works on Bunker Hill ! The Yankees are attacking our works on Bunker Hill !"

At first the people thought it was part of the play ; but when General Howe ordered, " Officers to your posts ! "

"UNDER THIS TREE WASHINGTON FIRST TOOK COMMAND OF THE AMERICAN ARMY, JULY 3d, 1775,"

they began to realize that the play had indeed come to a sudden end. I fancy the hall was cleared quickly, indeed; and it was not many days before the British troop found that Washington's sword was not so rusty as they had thought; at any rate it was able to flash an idea into the British general's eye which made him think it worth while, not many days later, to take himself and his troops out of the town.

At last the provisions had run so low it seemed to General Howe, who was then in command, that the best thing to do was to leave the city while there was a chance. Then, too, Washington had begun to fortify Dorchester Heights; and General Howe feared that soon his escape would be cut off. And so, after stealing all the blankets and woolen and linen in the city, after spiking their cannon and throwing it into the harbor — doing, in short, all the mischief they could, they marched away from the city of Boston. And even as they marched out, they scattered all about the entrance to the city little irons, with sharp points sticking out in all directions. These irons were called "crow's feet," and they scattered them about that the colonists, when they entered the city, might tread upon them and so disable their feet.

The people of Boston had been shut in all this time with the British and the disloyal Tories; and you can imagine how glad they were when they saw Washington marching in at the head of his army.

SIGNING THE DECLARATION OF INDEPENDENCE.

NAMES OF PERSONS WHO SIGNED THE DECLARATION OF INDEPENDENCE.
COPY OF THEIR SIGNATURES — CAN YOU READ THEM?

## DECLARATION OF INDEPENDENCE.

At the beginning of the war the colonists had not expected to be free from British rule; indeed they did not wish to be. All they did ask was that they might be treated fairly. But since they had begun to fight, they grew more and more convinced that now nothing less than perfect independence of the mother-country ought to satisfy them.

Then the leading men of the colonies met together at Philadelphia to draw up a writing, in which they declared themselves no longer subject to English rule. Five men, Thomas Jefferson, Benjamin Franklin, John Adams, Roger Sherman and Robert Livingstone, were appointed to write it out; and when this was done every man in the Congress signed it.

It had been agreed that as soon as the Declaration was adopted the old bell-man should ring the big " Liberty-bell " that hung in the tower of the old State House, in order that the great throng of people outside might know it. This, as I suppose you all know, happened July 4, 1776.

The old bell-man had taken his place up in the tower, and had told his little grandson to tell him when the time came to ring the bell.

Messengers were sent in every direction to tell the news in every village and town; the boys lit fires, the cannons blazed, and everywhere the people — men, women, and children, tried in every way to show their joy that they were now all to stand shoulder to shoulder, *a free nation*.

Ask your teacher to let you learn this poem about the bell ringing of that day, to read in concert; and if you are one-half as patriotic as the boys and girls then were, I'm sure you'll read it in such a way that the teacher will think "Independence day has come again."

> There was tumult in the city,
>   In the quaint old Quaker town,
> And the streets were rife with people,
>   Pacing restless up and down ;—
> People gathering at corners,
>   Where they whispered each to each,
> And the sweat stood on their temples,
>   With the earnestness of speech.
>
> " Will they do it? "   ' Dare they do it? "
>   " Who is speaking? "   " What's the news? "
> " What of Adams? "   " What of Sherman? "
>   " Oh, God grant they won't refuse ! "
> " Make some way there ! "   " Let me nearer ! "
>   " I am stifling ! "   " Stifle then !
> When a nation's life's at hazard,
>   We've no time to think of men ! "

So they beat against the portal,
   Man and woman, maid and child;
And the July sun in heaven
   On the scene looked down and smiled,
The same sun that saw the Spartan
   Shed his patriot blood in vain,
Now beheld the soul of freedom
   All unconquer'd rise again.

See! See! The dense crowd quivers
   Through all its lengthy line,
As the boy beside the portal
   Looks forth to give the sign!
With his small hands upward lifted,
   Breezes dallying with his hair,
Hark! with deep, clear intonation,
   Breaks his young voice on the air.

Hushed the people's swelling murmur,
   List, the boy's exultant cry!
"Ring!" he shouts, "Ring, Grandpa,
   Ring, O, ring for Liberty!"
And straightway at the signal,
   The old bellman lifts his hand,
And sends the good news, making
   Iron music through the land.

How they shouted! What rejoicing!
   How the old bell shook the air,
Till the clang of freedom ruffled
   The calm, gliding Delaware!
How the bonfires and the torches
   Illumed the night's repose,
And from the flames like fabled Phœnix,
   Our glorious Liberty arose!

That old bell now is silent,
   And hushed its iron tongue,
But the spirit it awakened,
   Still lives — forever young.
And when we greet the smiling sunlight,
   On the fourth of each July,
We'll ne'er forget the bellman,
   Who, betwixt the earth and sky,
Rang out OUR INDEPENDENCE,
   Which, please God, *shall never die!*

---

## THE HISTORY OF OUR FLAG.

The old British flag which had once been so dear to the colonists, and which they now so hated, was pulled down from every place, and the new American flag hoisted in its place. For the colonists had long ago learned that no peace with England was possible. They had once offered a petition to the king, in which they had asked that peace might be restored on certain conditions. This petition, the king would not even hear read; and so the colonists had long known that their only hope lay in face-to-face battle with the English troops.

And now that they had declared their independence of England, surely they would no longer bear an English flag.

PINE TREE FLAG.

At the beginning of the war, there had been in use a variety of flags. One of the very first was the "Pine Tree" flag. This was used first in the Massachusetts colony. It had a white ground, a tree in the middle, and the motto, "Appeal to Heaven." Next, a flag was made having upon it thirteen stripes of red and white to represent the thirteen colonies. It had, however, the British "Union-Jack," as it was called, in the corner. But when the Declaration of Independence came, then, said the colonists, we must have a truly American flag; for now we are the American nation.

Congress voted, June, 17, 1777, "that the flag of the thirteen United States be thirteen stripes, alternate red and white, and the Union be thirteen white stars in the blue field."

The first truly American flag was hoisted by Paul Jones over an American ship-of-war. This flag was made by Philadelphia women, and I am sure they must have been proud to have done their part in the raising of the first American flag.

It was intended that, as time went on and the country grew, a new stripe should be added for each new State; but later, when the growth of the country caused the flag to become too wide, it was decided to return to the thirteen original stripes, and let a new star be added for each new State. And thus it is that our flag to-day shows thirteen stripes of red and white, while in its blue field, where the "Union Jack" used to stand, are — what little boy or girl can tell me how many stars there are on our flag to-day?

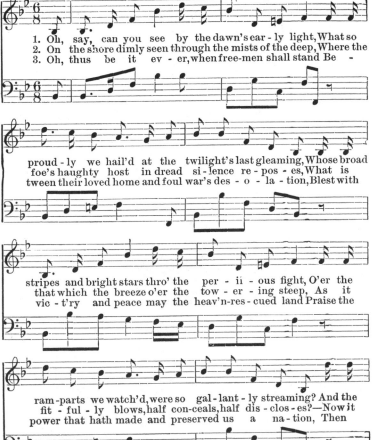

1. Oh, say, can you see by the dawn's ear - ly light, What so
2. On the shore dimly seen through the mists of the deep, Where the
3. Oh, thus be it ev - er, when free-men shall stand Be -

proud - ly we hail'd at the twilight's last gleaming, Whose broad
foe's haughty host in dread si - lence re - pos - es, What is
tween their loved home and foul war's des - o - la - tion, Blest with

stripes and bright stars thro' the per - il - ous fight, O'er the
that which the breeze o'er the tow - er - ing steep, As it
vic - t'ry and peace may the heav'n-res - cued land Praise the

ram - parts we watch'd, were so gal - lant - ly streaming? And the
fit - ful - ly blows, half con-ceals, half dis - clos - es?—Now it
power that hath made and preserved us a na - tion, Then

# OUR FLAG IS THERE.

This song was written by an officer of the American Navy during the war of 1812.

1. Our flag is there! Our flag is there! We'll hail it with three
2. That flag withstood the bat-tle's roar, With foemen stout, with

loud huzzahs! Our flag is there! Our flag is there! Be -
foemen brave; Strong hands have sought that flag to low'r, And

hold the glorious stripes and stars! Stout hearts have fought for
found a speed-y wa-'try grave! That flag is known on

that bright flag, Strong hands sustained it mast head high, And
ev-'ry shore, The stan-dard of a gal-lant band, A -

Oh! to see how proud it waves, Brings tears of joy in ev-'ry eye.
like unstain'd in peace or war, It floats o'er freedom's happy land.

# A PETTY TYRANT.

In the early days of the Revolution, there was a British officer, General Prescott, stationed at Newport. Although his name was the same, he was a very different man from the one we heard of at Bunker Hill. He was a mean sort of a man, and seemed to think that frightening children, and threatening women, were quite brave things to do.

He demanded that every man who met him should take off his hat to him as he passed. As the people of Newport were entirely at his mercy, many of them obeyed him.

One day, a good old Quaker came along. "Take off that hat," shouted Prescott.

"I take off my hat to no man," said the Quaker.

"Knock off that old fool's hat," said Prescott to one of his companions. And threatening and swearing, Prescott passed on, resolved to get his revenge in some way on the Quaker.

He could think of nothing that would grieve the old man more than to take away from him a pair of horses of which he was very fond. Beautiful black horses they were, as gentle and loving with the old Quaker as kittens.

The very next morning Prescott sent a detachment of soldiers to take these horses. Of course there was nothing to do but to give them up. Whatever the cruel General did with them was never known, but that afternoon the good old Quaker found one lying by the roadside, dying. The old man knelt down beside him, took his head into his lap, sobbing like a child over his four-footed friend. The poor horse tried to lift his head to look into his old master's face, and, with one great shudder, dropped back dead.

At another time, this Prescott wanted a sidewalk in front of his house; and so, instead of going to work to collect the stones honestly and build his sidewalk, he ordered his men to take up the doorsteps of the houses in the neighborhood and build one for him.

The people of Newport declared they would endure him no longer; and so one night, Colonel Barton, one of the patriots of Newport, planned to surprise the General and take him prisoner. Prescott was then staying at the house of a Quaker a little outside of the town.

Quietly they crept up to the house and entered. "Where is Prescott's room?" said Barton to the Quaker. The Quaker pointed directly overhead, and up the stairs they dashed, a little negro boy Jack, who hated the General well, leading the way. Bang went the tough little woolley head of Jack against the door of the chamber and open it flew.

Prescott sprang up in bed as they entered; but there was no chance for escape. His aid in another room, hearing the noise, jumped out of the window to give the alarm, but was instantly captured by the men below. Barton ordered the General to rise, and go with them. He begged

for time to dress.   But delay was dangerous.   Throwing a
cloak about him, they took him in his shirt, telling him that
on the other side of the bay he would have time to dress at
his leisure.   The rest of the party who had remained on
guard outside, formed around the prisoners ; and as stealthily
as they came they made their way back to the boats.   Once
again with muffled oars they passed by the frigates, the men
chuckling to themselves as they heard the sentry's cry of
' All's well ! ' and thinking how angry they would be when,
a little later, they learned than all was ill."

He was carried to Washington's camp and made a prisoner.   It is said that while on the way to Washington, he
was so rude to the wife of a Connecticut innkeeper that her
husband gave him a sound horse-whipping.

---

## THE LEADEN STATUE.

There had been so much resistance to the Stamp Act
before the Revolution that England repealed it not long
after.   The colonists were overjoyed at the news, because
they thought it meant that the English King had decided to
deal fairly with the colonists in the future.   The Sons of
Liberty in New York City, in an excess of joy, cast a leaden
statue of the King, and set it up in the Bowling Green.

Hardly was it in place when news came that the English government had passed another law, more unjust if possible than the Stamp Act; and that they were going to send troops over to take possession of the harbors of the principal cities. And when, in the following spring, troops stationed themselves on Staten Island, the fury of these Sons of Liberty knew no bounds.

Then, when, at last, came the Declaration of Independence, read to them by Washington himself, they thronged through the streets shouting "Liberty! Liberty!"

"Down with the statue of England's King," cried one; and in an instant the air rang with the cries of "Down with the statue! down with the King!"

Rushing to the Green, they tore it down; and, whooping and dancing like wild Indians, they hacked it in pieces.

"Give us the lead," cried a Daughter of Liberty, "and we women will make it into bullets to shoot these British tyrants."

"Yes! yes!" cried the mob; give the lead to the Daughters of Liberty."

And so the Daughters of Liberty, without so much noise perhaps, but with just as much patriotism, went to work making the lead up into bullets. It is said that the names of the women who made the largest number were placed on record. Report says that Mrs. Marvin made 6058; Laura Marvin 8370; Mary Marvin 10,790 and Ruth Marvin 11,592.

## "FREE AND EQUAL."

When the affair known as the "Boston Tea Party" occurred, Cynthia Smith was five years old. Her home was in Charleston, and she helped in many ways when her father sent all his rice to the North, as he was obliged to, because England had shut up our harbor by what is known as the "Boston Port Bill." Two years later, she saw, with aching heart, four of her brothers go to the war; and, eager to help the cause, she learned in time to spin, to weave, and to knit for the brave soldiers. The only pleasure she had was with a pretty red and white calf that her father had given her; and when the Declaration of Independence was signed she named her pet "Free-'n-Equal." Through all the dreary days and months which followed, Cynthia grew more and more fond of her friend. Still she longed to go herself and fight for her country. Finally her father and one remaining brother left home to join General Gates' army. During this time, great damage was done to the Southern homes by the British soldiers. Cynthia was ready to protect her home and mother, come what might. But one day, on returning from an errand, she was dismayed to find that the British soldiers had carried off "Free-n'-Equal." It did not take long, however, for Cynthia to decide what she would do. Off she started at once for the headquarters of Lord Cornwallis. Hurrying over three miles of hot, dusty road, she gained entrance to the great General's room. A feast was being held just then ; but once in his presence, it would not do to give up ; so, summoning all her courage, she told him that his soldiers had stolen her cow, and that she had come to take her back again. Lord Cornwallis was much attracted towards the "sturdy little rebel" as he called her, and promised to have "Free-'n-Equal" returned to her at once. Before the little girl went back home with her pet, the General patted her on her head, told her she was a brave little woman, and gave her a pair of silver knee-buckles. These buckles are still in the hands of the descendants of Cynthia Smith, and they are, and justly too, very proud of them and of their grandmother, once the little Cynthia.

------

## An Anecdote of Washington.

During the Revolution, George Washington was one day riding by a group of soldiers who did not know him. They were busily engaged in raising a beam to the top of some military works. It was a difficult task, and often the corporal's voice could be heard shouting, " *Now* you have it !" "All ready ! *Pull!*" Washington quietly asked the corporal why he didn't turn to and help them. "Sir," angrily replied the corporal, "do you realize that *I* am the *corporal?*"

Washington politely raised his hat, saying, "I did *not* realize it. Beg pardon Mr. Corporal; then dismounting, he himself fell to work and helped the men till the beam was raised. Before leaving he turned to the corporal, and, wiping the perspiration from his face, said, "If ever you need assistance like this again, call upon Washington, your cammander-in-chief, and I will come." The confused corporal turned red, then white, as he realized that this was Washington himself to whom he had been so pompous; and we hope he learned a lesson of true greatness.

## LYDIA DARRAH SAVES GEN. WASHINGTON.

At one time, General Washington was very near being attacked by the British army, and his army would very likely have been totally destroyed had not a brave Quaker woman, Lydia Darrah, risked her life to warn him of his danger.

One night, one of the British officers who was stationed in her house, ordered her to see that her family were abed and asleep at a certain hour, and to admit General Howe very quietly, show him to the officer's apartment, and be ready to let him out just as quietly, when he should be ready to go.

Lydia was suspicious. She felt that some treachery was

on foot. So when General Howe was safely in his officer's apartment, she took off her shoes, crept softly up-stairs, and listened at the keyhole. There she heard them plan to surprise Washington, and take him and his whole army. When she had heard enough she went trembling to bed, and was apparently so sound asleep that the officer had to knock again and again when he came to rouse her to let General Howe out of the house.

Next day good Mrs. Darrah got a pass from General Howe to go to mill and get some flour ground, outside the lines of the army in Philadelphia. Off she walked with a bag of wheat in her arms, to the outposts of the patriot army, twenty-five miles away. Meeting an officer there, she told her story, and begged the Americans to put Washington at once on his guard. When Howe's forces marched toward White Marsh with the greatest secrecy, they found such excellent preparations to receive them, that they turned round and marched back again, without striking a blow.

The officer questioned Mrs. Darrah. "Were any of your family awake the night General Howe was here?" "Not a soul," she answered. "Then the walls of this house must have heard our plans," he said, "for some one reported them to the rebel Washington. When we got to White Marsh, he was all ready for us, and we had the pleasure of marching back like a parcel of fools."

## Washington's Christmas Surprise.

*School in concert.*

> All hail, thou blessed Christmas time,
> When joy-bells ring their merry chime!
> The time of gifts and sweet surprise,
> Of smiling lips and beaming eyes.

*(Pupil enters and recites the following:)*

> Not enough of Christmas joys
> Without a Christmas story, boys?
> Methinks I've just the one for you,
> And what is better still, 'tis true.

> Then lend your ears and bright young eyes
> While I recount that grand surprise
> Of Washington's long years ago,
> Amid the Winter's cold and snow.

> 'Twas in our country's stern old fight
> For Independence and the right.
> Within your minds the date well fix —
> 'Twas Christmas night of seventy-six.

> Our army, footsore, weary, sad,
> In numbers few, ill-fed, ill-clad,
> And fearing much the English foe,
> Were spending days in want and woe.

> The Hessian camp was all aglow,
> And freely there the red wines flow;
> Their caution on this Christmas night
> In revelling's had taken flight.

> To Washington was known the way,
> The Germans oft spent Christmas day,

WASHINGTON CROSSING THE DELAWARE.

And so, while they were free from cares,
He planned to take them unawares.

The Delaware between them rolled,
The night was stormy, dark, and cold,
The floating ice blocked up their way,
But on they pressed, and morning gray

Beheld them on the Trenton side
Hard-spent. but filled with honest pride;
Then on the Hessian camp they fall,—
A thousand prisoners take in all.

With booty, prisoners and all,
They follow at their leader's call;
Again they cross the river wide,
And reach the Pennsylvania side.

*Voice.*   A brilliant act !   A brilliant thought!
And one with mighty issues fraught!
And unto Washington so wise,
We're debtors for that grand surprise.

*Voice.*   A record of that daring deed,
Just in his country's hour of need,
Will ever live in song and fame,
While lives the hero's honored name,
And memory keeps, in pictures rare,
That " Crossing on the Delaware."

*All.*   When Christmas fires send out their glow
Across the pure, untrodden snow,
Let thought go back to that far time,
When rang the bells no merry chime;
But one brave heart, 'neath wintry skies,
Planned out this Christmas-day surprise.

                              —M. LIZZIE STANLEY.

# WASHINGTON'S CHRISTMAS GIFT TO THE AMERICAN ARMY.

Washington's army had for some time had nothing but defeat. This, of course, was very encouraging to the British side. There were only about three thousand men with him, and these were suffering from cold and hunger.

Washington felt that a bold stroke must be made, and that too very soon. He knew that there were encamped just across the Delaware, a body of Hessian troops, who had been hired and sent over here by the English government to fight against the colonists.

Washington knew the ways of these Hessians; and he was quite sure that they would spend Christmas day (1776) in a great celebration, and very likely would be "off guard" in the evening.

It was a terrible night. The sleet and rain were pouring down; it was bitterly cold, and the river so full of broken ice that, in the inky darkness, it seemed almost impossible to get across. But Washington was brave, his soldiers believed in him, and so they struggled on.

It was four o'clock in the morning when the last boat-load of men reached the Trenton shore. They crept silently along the bank to where the Hessians lay, tired out with Christmas revelry, and thus burst suddenly upon their unsuspecting enemy. It was a glorious victory. The Hessians were captured almost before they could rub their eyes open. Washington lost hardly ten men in all and captured almost one thousand Hessians, besides cannon, guns, and ammunition. The Hessians were sent off for winter-quarters into central Pennsylvania, where they found many German settlers, who treated them kindly and spoke their own language. They had a very comfortable time there, and always spoke of Washington as "a very good rebel." And so ended with a success at last the year of 1776, which had for some months looked so dark and dismal to the American army.

## VALLEY FORGE.

All through the winter of 1777 and '78 the British and the American armies lay only twenty miles apart. The red-coats with their commander, General Howe, were quartered in Philadelphia. There they were entertained by the Tories who gave parties, and balls and dinners, and did all in their power to make the winter a pleasant one for these British soldiers.

Twenty miles away, in a rocky, desolate, mountain gorge known as Valley Forge, Washington had led his army from White Marsh. When he went there in bitter December weather, his men, shoeless and almost naked, had marked their way with blood from their bare feet. They reached the valley, and for want of tents were obliged to cut down trees and build huts of logs for shelter from the cold. Congress had no money to pay the men, no money to buy them food. For days and days together, during this winter, they had no bread and lived upon salt pork alone. They sickened with hunger and cold, and there was no money to buy medicines, no comfortable hospitals where they could be nursed. They were ragged and without shoes.

It was a terrible winter for them all. Washington's brave heart ached, and sometimes was very heavy as he saw his men starving, and freezing, and dying. It seemed almost as if the cause of the colonists must be given up. But you have heard the saying that " it is always darkest just before day." And so it proved just now ; for in the spring word came from France that aid was to be sent them from that country. When the British heard this, they would have been very glad to make peace with the colonists. Indeed, messengers were sent over from England with very liberal offers — offers which, before the war, the colonists would have accepted ; but that time was past now. Then these messengers tried to bribe some of the officers in the patriot army. One man, General Reed of Pennsylvania, was offered ten thousand guineas and distinguished honors if he would exert his influence to effect a reconciliation. "I am not worth purchasing," said the honest patriot, " but such as I am, the king of Great Britain is not rich enough to buy me."

## EMILY GEIGER.

'Twas in days of the Revolution,—
  Dark days were they and drear,—
And by Carolina firesides
  The women sat in fear;
For the men were away at the fighting,
  And sad was the news that came,
That the battle was lost; and the death-list
  Held many a loved one's name.

When as heart-sore they sat round the camp-fires,
   " What ho !   Who'll volunteer
To carry a message to Sumter?"
   A voice rang loud and clear.
There was a sudden silence,
   But not a man replied ;
They knew too well of the peril
   Of one who dared that ride.


Outspoke then Emily Geiger,
   With a rich flush on her cheek, —
" Give me the message to be sent ;
   I am the one you seek.
For I am a Southern woman ;
   And I'd rather do and dare
Than sit by a lonely fireside,
   My heart gnawed through with care."


They gave her the precious missive ;
   And on her own good steed
She rode away, 'mid the cheers of the men,
   Upon her daring deed.
And away through the lonely forests,
   Steadily galloping on,
She saw the sun sink low in the sky,
   And in the west go down.


" Halt ! — or I fire ! "   On a sudden
   A rifle clicked close by.
" Let you pass?   Not we, till we know you are
   No messenger nor spy."
" She's a Whig, — from her face — I will wager,"

Swore the officer of the day.
" To the guard-house, and send for a woman
To search her without delay."

No time did she lose in bewailing ;
    As the bolt creaked in the lock,
She quickly drew the precious note
    That was hidden in her frock.
And she read it through with hurried care,
    Then ate it, piece by piece,
And calmly set her down to wait
    Till time should bring release.

They brought her out in a little,
    And set her on her steed,
With many a rude apology,
    For their discourteous deed.
On, on, once more through the forest black,
    The good horse panting strains,
Till the sentry's challenge, " Who comes there ? "
    Tells that the end she gains.

Ere an hour, in the camp of Sumter
    There was hurrying to and fro.
" Saddle and mount, saddle and mount ! "
    The bugles shrilly blow.
" Forward trot ! " and the long ranks wheel,
    And into the darkness glide :
Long shall the British rue that march
    And Emily Geiger's ride.

## MASSACRE OF WYOMING.

One of the saddest events of this sad year, 1778, was the massacre of Wyoming.

Wyoming has a quiet little village in the Wyoming valley along the Susquehanna river.   These Wyoming settlers were very loyal people ;— hardly a family among them but had sent a dear father or son to the army.   All around them were the Tories, who looked upon this peaceful little village with fierce hate.

One summer evening, these Tories got together six hundred Indians, and with howls and yells, shouts and war-whoops, all swept down upon the little village.

The women and children, frightened, hurried within the walls of " Fort Forty," the only stronghold they owned.

One hardly dares think how much more terrible still this might have been had not one Zebulon Butler, a brave young soldier, chanced to be home on a furlough.

He quickly mustered all the old men and boys into a little army.   Then, finding their only hope lay in rushing forth to meet their foe in open field, they left the fort and went bravely out, led by their brave leader.

It was a brief, deadly encounter.   The foe, five times their number, broke savagely upon them.   When at last the little band gave way, the Indians and the Tories, one hardly less blood-thirsty than the other, pursued them with unrelenting fury.

There is no more brutal picture in all history than this massacre of the peaceful, loyal people of Wyoming. A description of it, even, is too horrible for children's ears. So we will ask you to read Campbell's poem of " Gertrude of Wyoming." It is a famous poem, one you will often come across, by and by, in your school-life ; and it is well you should remember what it has to do with the early history of your own people.

MONUMENT ERECTED AT WYOMING.

## THE SURRENDER OF BURGOYNE.

In this war of the Revolution you will always hear a great deal about *the surrender of Burgoyne* and *the surrender of Cornwallis.* These two British generals were at the head of large armies, and had arranged most extensive plans for series of battles, which, had they been successful, would have ruined completely the American army ; and instead of the grand history of independence, of progress and of growth which we now have, there would have been I fear, a very sad ending for the Revolution, and a history sadder still of the years that followed.

This General Burgoyne had been sent over from England with an army of "picked men," great stores of firearms, and some of the finest brass cannon that had ever at that time been made.

I fancy the colonists would have been much more afraid of this general and his soldiers, had Burgoyne not done something, as soon as he reached this county, which was so ridiculous that it made the American officers and soldiers roar with laughter when they heard of it.

You see General Burgoyne was a very pompous sort of a man, much given to strutting and bragging. While he was in England, he had written two or three comic plays for the theatre ; and had, I suspect, quite a high opinion of his own composition ; for as soon as ever he had settled himself here in America, he wrote out a long, long proclamation, in which he talked to the colonists much as a big bully of a boy might talk to a very little boy.

He promised a great many things to the Americans if they would lay down their arms and surrender at once ; but if they did not, there was no end to the awful things he threatened to do ; — he would destroy their cities, he would cut their throats, he would let the Indians loose upon them, indeed, he would, judging from his threats, hardly leave the earth for them to walk upon. Now, the colonists believed that the stillest waters run deepest ; and so, although Burgoyne was indeed a great general, and had a powerful army, the colonists were sharp enough to see that there was a great deal of wind and bluster about this Englishman after all. Then, too, he wound up this proclamation of his by signing his name with ten or fifteen big sounding titles, expecting that the colonists would surely look with great reverence upon these. But the patriots had now outgrown any reverence they might once have for English titles, and the newspapers all over the country made all sorts of fun of this proclamation. And said it was a bigger comedy than those he had written in England.

Burgoyne's plan was to come down from Canada into New York State, get possession of the Hudson River, and so hem in the colonies of New Hampshire, Vermont,

Massachusetts, Connecticut and Rhode Island, that they would be compelled to surrender.

As you already know, Burgoyne failed in his plan in the end ; but it was a terrible campaign for the patriots for all that. For Burgoyne engaged the Indians on his side ; and wherever the Indians fought, you know there was scalping, and burning, and murder on every side.

At one time, when General Herkimer was on his way with a company of about eight hundred patriots to help defend a poorly garrisoned fort, a party of these Indians, aided by some cowardly Tories fell upon them and butchered them most savagely. Brave old General Herkimer fought like a tiger. When he had been shot in both legs, and could no longer stand, he sat down upon a stump, still cheering his men on, while with a rifle, he fired at the enemy as long as he could pull the trigger.

At another time, General Burgoyne sent a detachment of his men to attack the colonial army at Bennington. General Stark had just arrived there with an army from the New Hampshire militia. Now, General Stark's wife, Molly, was a patriotic woman, and was well known and highly respected in her husband's army. And so, when the British appeared, General Stark said, "Boys, the British are coming ; there's a hard battle ahead ; beat them we must, or to-morrow morning Molly Stark will be a widow."

It was indeed a close fight ; but success attended the

army of the general whose wife's name he had made the
watchword.

---

## SARATOGA.

There was another terrible battle this time at Saratoga, in
which General Gates succeeded in so breaking up Burgoyne's army that this proud British general was obliged to
surrender.

Both generals had fought bravely and skilfully; and
although they were enemies in battle, they respected each
other as men; and when, after the surrender, Burgoyne
gave up his sword to Gates, he did so very courteously, saying, "The fortunes of war, General Gates, have made me
your prisoner."

General Gates, taking the sword, said with equal polite-
ness, "I shall always be glad to testify, General Burgoyne,
that it was through no fault of yours that it happened so."

I am afraid the newspapers again printed many jokes
about the defeated Burgoyne, as they recalled the extrava-
gant threats he had made at the beginning of his campaign.

His people, too, in England blamed him severely, which
I think was rather unjust; for, in spite of all, he was a brave
and skilful soldier; the only trouble was that he was on the

wrong side of the truth, and the wrong side seldom succeeds in any battle.

---

## THE HALF-WITTED TORY BOY.

At the very beginning Burgoyne was upset in his plans by a half-witted boy. To be sure, this was no credit to the boy, nor was it any discredit to Burgoyne; still, in the later days of the war, when Burgoyne had been conquered by the Americans, and had been made to surrender, the colonists liked now and then to recall this little story as a joke.

St. Leger had been sent by Burgoyne to take a certain fort. Knowing this, Arnold was sent by the American general to hold the same fort against the attack. How the battle might have ended had Arnold and St. Leger met, we cannot tell, but, as the story goes, this is the way Arnold won the fort.

He had with him as a prisoner a half-witted boy. He had been taken from some Tory family very likely; for he would not or could not understand that he was in the hands of the Whigs, and so would keep saying over and over in his foolish way, "I Tory! I Tory!"

As the little fellow was homesick and miserable, Arnold was struck with the idea that perhaps he could make some

use of him by offering him his freedom.   So calling him to
him he said, "My young lad, would you like to go home?"

The poor little fellow jumped about and uttered some
strange sounds that meant to express his joy at the thought.

Then Arnold explained to him that if he would go to the
camp of St. Leger and tell him that a grea-a-at b-i-ig army
of Americans was coming to attack him, he should be given
his liberty.

The boy understood, and away he went.   He cut his
clothes full of round holes to represent bullet holes, and
rushed breathless into St. Leger's camp.

"What is it, boy?" where are you from? who are you?"
asked the British officers, frightened at his appearance.

I cannot tell you how he did it; but he managed to
make St. Leger believe that a terrible army was bearing
down upon him and that he had better escape while he
could.   When St. Leger asked him how many there were,
he pointed to the leaves of the trees, as if to say no one
could count them.   The result was that St. Leger and his
men took to flight, not even taking time to take down their
tents or pack their supplies.

They say, "All things are fair in war"—if so, I suppose
this must have been fair.   How does it seem to you little
boys and little girls?   You will have to talk this over with
your teacher, I think.

GENERAL FRANCIS MARION.

## THE FOX OF THE SOUTHERN SWAMP.

There was one brave patriot working away in the swampy country in South Carolina. This man was General Marion; and so wise was he, and so brave, and succeeded in stealing such marches upon the enemies in this southern district, that he was called the "fox of the southern swamp." I shall not try to tell you of the successful raids he made, and the successful battles he fought, because battles all sound pretty much alike to little folks, and you might grow tired of hearing of them. If I can tell you some of the stories of those times which will help you to understand the kind of men and women these patriots were, how brave they were, and how much they were willing to suffer for the cause which seemed to them right, I know your teacher will be better satisfied than she would be to hear you repeat like parrots the names and dates of all the battles in our whole history.

This General Marion had a camp in a swamp, among the forests and tangled grasses and mosses — a place so hidden and so hard to enter, that no one cared to attempt an attack upon him. From this place Marion and his men used to march forth to battle. At one time a British officer was brought into this camp to talk with Marion about some prisoners. After they had arranged matters, Marion invited the young officer to dine with him. The officer accepted; but when he was taken to the "mess-room," and saw only a pine log for a table, on which were heaped nothing but baked potatoes, he asked in astonishment,

"Is this all you have for dinner?" "This is all," answered General Marion, "and we thought ourselves fortunate in having more potatoes than usual, when we had a visitor to dine with us."

"You must have good pay to make up for such living," said the officer.

"On the contrary," answered Marion, "I have never received a dollar, nor has one of my men."

"What on earth are you fighting for?"

"For the love of liberty," answered the hero.   The story says that the young officer went back to Charleston and resigned his position in the English army, saying he would not fight against men who fought from such motives, and were willing to endure such hardships.

---

## SONG OF MARION'S MEN.

Our band is few, but true and tried, our leader frank and bold;
The British soldier trembles when Marion's name is told;
Our fortress is the good greenwood, our tent the cypress tree;
We know the forest round us, as seamen know the sea.
We know its walls of thorny vines, its glades of reedy grass,
Its safe and silent islands within the dark morass.

Woe to the English soldiery that little dread us near!
On them shall light at midnight a strange and sudden fear;
When, waking to their tents on fire, they grasp their arms in vain,
And they who stand to face us are beat to earth again;

And they who fly in terror deem a mighty host behind,
And hear the tramp of thousands upon the hollow wind.


Then sweet the hour that brings release from danger and from toil!
We talk the battle over and share the battle's spoil;
The woodland rings with laugh and shout, as if a hunt were up,
And woodland flowers were gathered to crown the soldier's cup.
With merry songs we mock the wind that in the pine-top grieves.
And slumber sound and sweetly on beds of oaken leaves


Well knows the fair and friendly moon the band that Marion
    leads —
The glitter of their rifles, the scampering of their steeds.
'Tis life to guide the fiery barb across the moonlit plain;
'Tis life to feel the night-wind that lifts his tossing mane.
A moment in the British camp — a moment and away
Back to the pathless forest before the peep of day.


Grave men they are by broad Santee, grave men with hoary hairs,
Their hearts are all with Marion, for Marion are their prayers.
And lovely ladies greet our band with kindest welcoming,
With smiles like those of summer and tears like those of spring.
For them we wear these rusty arms, and lay them down no more,
Till we have driven the Britons forever from our shore.

                          — BRYANT.

## THE WOMEN OF SOUTH CAROLINA.

The women of South Carolina were not one step behind the men in bravery and patriotic spirit.

In a certain battle at Cowpens — not a very romantic name — a certain General Tarleton was totally defeated by an American officer, Colonel Washington. General Tarleton, who was, I think, not much of a gentleman, used to seize every opportunity to sneer at Colonel William Washington whenever a certain patriotic woman, a great admirer of the brave young Washington, was present.

Now, as Tarleton bore a wound which young Washington had given him, and had, moreover, been chased like a puppy from the battlefield, one would think that Tarleton's good taste would have prevented him from saying much about it ; but Tarleton had not very exquisite taste, I think.

"I should like to see this young friend of yours," said Tarleton one day to this lady ; "I hear he is a very common, mean-looking man."

"If you had taken time to look *behind* you at Cowpens, General Tarleton, you would have been sure to see him," returned the lady quickly.

One would suppose, after this sharp reply, that General Tarleton would have said no more against Colonel Washington, but only a few days later, at a large dinner, at which this same lady was present, General Tarleton again said, "I understand that this young Washington is a very ignorant man. I am told that he cannot even write his name."

"Possibly he cannot," said the lady, quick-witted as before; "but," continued she, pointing to General Tarleton's wounded arm, "he can make his *mark* as you yourself can testify."

Another story is told of a South Carolina woman who had seven sons in the patriotic army. One day, a British general stopped at her house, and tried to show her how much better it would be for her sons if they would only join the British army.

"Join the British army!" cried she. "Sooner than see one of my boys turn against his own country, would *I* go, this baby in my arms, and enlist under Marion's banner, and show my sons how to fight, and, if need be, *die*, for the freedom of this land of ours."

And these brave women of South Carolina not only encouraged their husbands and sons by brave words, but often acted the part of messengers in expeditions of trust and secrecy. Two brave women, whose husbands were in the army, disguised themselves in the dress of men, and captured two British soldiers, compelled them to give up the messages they were carrying, and bore them to General Greene, whose camp was not far distant.

## ISRAEL PUTNAM.

This brave general was born in Salem, Massachusetts, in 1718. He was only a farmer boy, and so had very little chance to learn the many things about the wide, wide world that you boys and girls are learning every day. He was a plucky little fellow though, and was the leader among the boys of his town in all sorts of things — mischief as well as other things I have no doubt.

At school he learned easily all there was to be taught him ; and if he knew nothing but the "three r's," that was not his fault, for that was all little folks were taught in those days.

Do you know what people mean when they speak of the "three r's?" Perhaps I shall not tell you the story just right, but this is something like the way it is told.

Once, in a country village, a school-board was holding a meeting. One man, rather more educated than the rest, arose and said, "I think, gentlemen, we might put a few more studies into our schools. I should like to see our boys and girls studying about the flowers and the stars; I should like to have them know about the different countries and the different people of this world. I move that a committee be appointed to see what can be done about making the course of study bigger, and better, and broader for our children."

Then a hot discussion followed. One man said it was all bosh; another said there was no need of knowing about countries or people that were thousands of miles away; another said he had no money to waste on such foolishness; another said the stars and flowers wouldn't help a boy to earn his bread and butter half as much as potatoes and squashes would. At last one man arose and said, "I don't care nothing about these new fangled notions and what's more I don't want to know about 'em. You and me was brought up in the deestrick school where we learned our readin' and 'ritin' and 'rithmetic. Mr. Chairman, move that we stick to the old way. The three 'r's' was good enough for me and it's good enough for my boys. Yes, sir! 'the three r's'— by that I mean 'readin', 'ritin' and 'rithmetic.''

Well, what has all this to do with Israel Putnam? Not very much after all, perhaps. Only to give you an idea of the the kind of schools there used to be in those days. It was to this sort of a school where they taught nothing but the "three r's" that Israel Putnam was sent to get his "larnin'" as his old father used to call it.

But, as I said before, he was a plucky boy, and took the lead in all sorts of sports. He could climb like a squirrel, run like a hare, leap like a frog. He could, in short, do all sorts of things that boys admire to do. He was very generous and just; but he wouldn't take an insult from any other boy if he could help himself.

One time, while yet quite a little lad, his father took him to Boston. As he stood admiring this new city, which to the little country boy looked so very, very big, another boy across the way called out, "Hello, country, aint it about time to milk the caows?"

Quick as a flash, the hot-headed lad fell upon the rude city boy, and gave him a thrashing that lasted him for many a day.

When Israel Putnam was a young man, living on a farm in Connecticut, he was very much troubled by wolf thieving.

Morning after morning he would find the number of his sheep and lambs lessened.

His neighbors, too, often found their chickens and hens gone, and only a few scattered feathers left to tell the story.

One morning finding a lamb which was to the farmer the pride of his flock among the missing, he started forth, gun in hand.

"There is a time," said Israel to his neighbors, "when even a wolf had better be taught that the way of transgressors is hard. I propose that we leave our farm work for to-day, and give this thief a good chase."

Several of the farmers, ready, I suspect for a good time as well as anxious to catch the wolf, joined in a party; and with Israel, who was always full of dry, "cute" sayings as we Yankees call it, at their head, they started out.

They were soon upon the track, and at last, with the aid of their keen-scented dogs, found the wolf's den.

It was a deep hollow in a rock, the opening of which was so small that the farmers could only enter one by by one crawling on their hands and knees.

"Now we've lost him," said one farmer.

"Let's smoke him out," said another. So they built a fire of leaves and brush just inside the cave; but no wolf appeared.

"Set the dogs upon him," said another farmer. But the dogs came skulking out yelping with pain.

"We're not going to be beaten in this way," said Putnam; "I'll go in there myself." And so, tying a rope round his legs, that the men might draw him out, he crawled slowly in, his gun in one hand, and a torch in the other.

He soon saw the eyes of the wolf glaring at him from a corner of the cave. Bang! went the gun, and half-blinded by the smoke and half deafened by the noise, Putnam was dragged out by the farmers. Reloading his gun, back he went and fired again — and again was he pulled out.

For the third time he entered, and finding the animal was dead he hauled her out by the ears, while his companions pulled him by the rope round his legs. His clothes were all torn off his back, and his face black with smoke and powder, but he had killed the wolf, and kept her skin as a trophy.

During the whole time of the Revolution, Israel Putnam was one of the foremost in every danger.

After one battle, he found that fourteen bullets had passed through his clothing, not one of which had injured him in the least. At another time when the fort was on fire he would not give up; but worked away at the burning timbers till his hands were burned nearly to a crisp.

At another time, he was taken prisoner by the Indians and bound to a tree. The bullets and the arrows flew on every side of him; one officer shot at him for the fun of it — but neither bullet or arrow struck him, although many of them struck the tree to which he was bound. It seemed indeed, as if he bore a " charmed life."

When the British began to land in New York, "Old Put"

led one division of the colonial army out of the city by way of the Hudson River road. He was to meet Washington not far up the river, and then together they intended to retreat.

Now it happened that at just the time Putnam was going *up* the river road, a British division was coming *down*. Mrs. Robert Murray, a good Quaker woman, who, although she did not believe in war and fighting, was nevertheless a staunch friend of the colonists, learned of the danger and resolved to save General Putnam.

The British red-coats, marching nearer and nearer, came until their advanced guard were at her very gate. Going forth to meet them, she saluted the officers and invited them to stop and lunch beneath her trees upon the lawn. The officers, tired and dusty with marching under the hot August sun, gladly accepted her seemingly generous hospitality.

She brought forth fresh bread with sweet golden butter, and gave them plenty of cold, foaming milk to drink, cake and fruits, everything that her house or garden could afford. She talked with them, showed them about her mansion, and in every way attempted to keep them pleasantly occupied until she was sure General Putnam had passed in the road below.

When at length the British division resumed its march, the sun had sunk nearer the west, the air was cooler, the

men were refreshed and rested — and, best of all, General
Putnam and his division had gone on far up the road and
out of sight.

At last, toward the end of the war, this daring general
was taken very ill.  So strong was his will, that, although
helpless and often in great pain, he lived on until the
Revolution was over.

He was bold and daring, had no mercy on his enemy in
battle, and when fighting, fought, as his soldiers used to say,
like a very wild-cat.

Still, for all that, he was generous and had as kind a
heart as ever beat.  He was not ashamed to be gentle with
his friends.  Every one who knew him loved him; and
when at the good old age of seventy-two, he died, he was
mourned by all.  Every honor was paid him by the country
he had so loved, and for which he had so bravely fought.

## BENJAMIN FRANKLIN.

One of the wisest men of the times was Benjamin Franklin. You have all heard about him I presume; there are so many stories of his boyhood, which no doubt, you have read in your reading book.

He was a very poor boy; that is, as far as money goes, but he had something in his little head that made him richer than the richest boy that ever scampered with him across Boston Common.

At ten years old he was taken from school to assist his father in his business of tallow-candler and soap-boiler.

"I was employed," he says, "in cutting wicks for the candles, attending the shop and going of errands."

Not liking this trade, however, Benjamin was apprenticed, at the age of twelve, to his brother James, a printer.

Here he staid for five years, but as he did not get along very well with his brother, he determined to start out and "seek his fortune."

Here is an account of his journey as told by himself: —

"My friend Collins agreed with the captain of a New York sloop for my passage to that city. So I sold some of my books to raise a little money, and as we had a fair wind, in three days I found myself in New York, near three hundred miles from home, a boy of but seventeen, without the least knowledge of any person in the place, and with very little money in my pocket.

"I offered my service to the printer in the place, old Mr. William Bradford. He could give me no employment, having little to do, but says he, "my son at Philadelphia has lately lost his principal man; if you go there, I believe he may employ you."

"Philadelphia was a hundred miles further; I set out, however, in a boat for Amboy, leaving my chest and things to follow me round by sea.

"From there I proceeded on foot, fifty miles to Burlington, where I was told I should find boats that would carry me the rest of the way to Philadelphia.

"It rained very hard all day. I was thoroughly soaked, and by noon a good deal tired; so I stopped at a poor inn, where I stayed all night, beginning now to wish that I had never left home.

"I cut so miserable a figure, too, that I found by the questions asked me, I was suspected to be some runaway servant, and in danger of being taken up on that suspicion. However, I proceeded the next day and got in the evening to Burlington.

"Walking there by the side of the river a boat came by,

which I found was going towards Philadelphia. They took me in, and, as there was no wind, we rowed all the way.

"We arrived at Philadelphia about nine o'clock on Sunday morning, and landed at the Market Street wharf.

"I have been the more particular in this description of my journey to Philadelphia, and shall be so of my first entry into that city, that you may in your mind compare such unlikely beginnings with the figures I have since made there. I was in my working dress, my best clothes being to come round by sea. I was dirty from my journey; my pockets were stuffed out with shirts and stockings, and I knew no soul, or where to look for lodging.

"I was fatigued with travelling, roving, and want of rest; I was very hungry; and my whole stock of cash consisted of a Dutch dollar, and about a shilling in copper.

"I walked up a street, gazing about, till, near the market-house, I met a boy with bread.

"I had made many a meal on bread, and, inquiring where he had bought it, I went immediately to the baker's he directed me to, in Second Street, and asked for a biscuit, intending such as we had in Boston; but they, it seems, were not made in Philadelphia.

"Then I asked for a threepenny loaf, and was told they had none such. So, not knowing the difference of money, or the greater cheapness or the names of his bread, I bade him give me threepenny-worth of any sort.

"He gave me, accordingly, three great, puffy rolls. I was surprised at the quantity, but took it, and, having no room in my pockets, walked off with a roll under each arm, and eating the other.

"Thus I went up Market Street as far as Fourth Street, passing by the door of Mr. Reed, my future wife's father; when she, standing at the door, saw me, and thought I made, as I certainly did, a most awkward and ridiculous appearance.

"I then turned and went down Chestnut Street, and part of Walnut Street, eating my roll all the way. Coming round, I found myself again at Market Street Wharf, near the boat I came in, to which I went for a draught of the river water; and being filled with one of my rolls, I gave the other two to a woman and her child who came down the river in the boat with us, and were waiting to go farther.

"Thus refreshed, I walked again up the street, which by this time had many clean-dressed people in it who were all walking the same way. I joined them, and thereby was led into a great meeting-house of the Quakers, near the market.

"I sat down among them, and, after looking round awhile and hearing nothing said, being very drowsy through labor and want of rest the preceding night, I fell fast asleep, and continued so till the meeting broke up, when one was kind

# Poor Richard, 1733.

## AN

# Almanack

### For the Year of Chrift

# 1733,

### Being the Firft after LEAP YEAR:

|  | Years |
|---|---|
| And makes fince the Creation | |
| By the Account of the Eaftern Greeks | 7241 |
| By the Latin Church, when ☉ ent. ♈ | 6932 |
| By the Computation of W.W. | 5742 |
| By the Roman Chronology | 5682 |
| By the Jewifh Rabbies | 5494 |

#### Wherein is contained

The Lunations, Eclipfes, Judgment of the Weather, Spring Tides, Planets Motions & mutual Afpects, Sun and Moon's Rifing and Setting. Length of Days. Time of High Water, Fairs, Courts, and obfervable Days Fitted to the Latitude of Forty Degrees and a Meridian of Five Hours Weft from London, but may without fenfible Error ferve all the adjacent Places, even from Newfoundland to South-Carolina

### By RICHARD SAUNDERS, Philom.

#### PHILADELPHIA.
Printed and fold by B. FRANKLIN, at the New Printing-Office near the Market.

enough to rouse me.    This was, therefore, the first house
I was in, or slept in, in Philadelphia."

It was this Franklin that made the wonderful first dis-
coveries in electricity ; and he made them by means of a
kite with a small thread, by which he found that he could
"bring down the lightning."

---

## "POOR RICHARD'S ALMANAC."

You should know about "Poor Richard's Almanac,"
children, for the same reason you should know about
"George Washington's Hatchet."

A hundred years ago, this was perhaps the foremost
book in American literature.    It was the work of our
lightning hero, Benjamin Franklin.    It was an almanac,
not unlike the "Old Farmer's Almanac" of to-day.    In
among the matter that is always to be found in almanacs,
Franklin scattered all sorts of "wise sayings" or proverbs.
To these he gave the name "Poor Richard's Sayings,"
Many of them you have heard over and over until very
likely you are tired of them.    Some of them, I know from
the experience of long ago, are very aggravating to children.    For example, isn't it enough to make any boy wish
Franklin had stuck by his printing press and his kite, and
let literature alone, to have mamma say, just as he is in

the midst of the most exciting chapter, "Come, Johnnie, it's time to go to bed.

> ' Early to bed and early to rise
> Makes a man healthy, wealthy and wise ? ' "

FRANKLIN AT HIS PRINTING PRESS.

"Poor Richard's Almanac" for 1734 says, in speaking of the eclipse for the year; "There will be but two; the first, April 22, the second, October 15 — both of the sun, and both, like old neighbor Scrape-all's generosity, invisible."

Franklin often put into his calendar "weather predictions;" but they were quite as likely to come out wrongly as do "Old Prob's" predictions now.

When he was criticised for the inaccuracy of his predictions, he said good-naturedly:

"However, *no* one but will allow that we always hit the day of the month. As for weather, I consider it will be of no service to anybody to know what weather is to be one thousand miles off; therefore, I always set down exactly the weather my reader will have wheresoever he may be *at the time*. We only ask an allowance of a few days and if there still be a mistake, set it down to the printer."

The almanac of 1738 has a scolding preface, which appears to be the work of Mistress Saunders. She says her husband had set out to visit an old star-gazer of his acquaintance on the Potomac, and left her the almanac, sealed, to send to the printer. She suspects some jests directed against her, bursts the seal, and plays havoc generally with the almanac. She says:

"Looking over the months, I find he has put in abundance of foul weather this year; and therefore I have scattered here and there, where I could find room, 'fair,' 'pleasant,' etc., for the poor women to dry their clothes in."

Franklin grew to be a highly educated man, and a very

gentlemanly man, too, for all he was so awkward and un-
gainly on his first morning in Philadelphia. Years later,
when he went to England and to France in behalf of his
country, his wit and his knowledge and his fine manners were
the delight of the Court. And this was a very fortunate
thing for America you may be sure, and for this reason, these
old European countries with all their elegance, and wealth,
and "blue blood," and Court society, had formed an idea
that Americans were all awkward clod-hoppers; "horny-
handed tillers of the soil," they were used to calling them, and
they had the idea, I suppose, that the country had not a single cultured, educated person upon its face. And so it was,
that when Franklin appeared before them, he carried every-
body by surprise; and many an Englishman and many a
Frenchman, who had supposed we knew nothing in America
except to dig in the earth, turned about and began to think
that perhaps we were "somebodies" over here after all.

Franklin was never dizzied by the flattering attention he
received in these countries. He never forgot that he was
there to plead for America; and plead he did, wisely and
well, many a time rendering her a service that she could
never repay.

In every position of honor, in every trying time when wisdom and caution were needed, Franklin was sure to be
called upon by his countrymen. And never did he fail them.

When at last he died, at the age of eighty-two, not only

did twenty thousand of his own countrymen meet to do him honor in America, but in the English and French courts as well, was every possible tribute paid to the memory of this great man.

BENJAMIN FRANKLIN'S TOMB.

## ARNOLD THE TRAITOR AND ANDRÉ THE SPY.

MAJOR ANDRÉ.

One of the most daring men in the patriotic army for a time was Benedict Arnold. He was brilliant, daring, but cowardly withal, mean-spirited, jealous and treacherous. His meaner qualities had not shown themselves very much in his military life, and, as he had really been very brave and had been of great service to the country, Washington put him in command at West Point, one of the most important military posts in the whole country.

But the mean-hearted Arnold had already planned to betray the post into the hands of the British; and Si: Henry Clinton, a British officer, had promised to give him £10,000 in English gold for his treacherous deed.

General Clinton sent a Major André to West Point to visit Arnold and make definite arrangements for the betrayal. He reached the American lines, met Arnold, and received papers from Arnold in which his whole plans were written. Putting these papers within his stockings, he started back to the British camp.

He had passed the American lines, and had reached

Tarrytown on the Hudson. Before night-fall he would be in the camp at New York, and the plan for the surrender would be in Clinton's hands. Almost free from apprehension of danger he rode on. Suddenly three men appeared in his path. Without producing his pass, he asked them, "Where do you belong?"

"Down below," answered one. "Down below" meant New York, and André was thrown off his guard by the answer. "I belong there also," he said. "I am a British officer on important business. Do not detain me."

"Then you are our prisoner," answered the men.

André then produced his pass, but as by his own confession he was a British officer, it availed nothing. He offered his watch, his purse, and more valuable than either, he offered to deliver to them next day a cargo of English dry goods if they would let him pass. They were unmoved by his bribes, and already had begun to search him. They searched pockets, saddle-bags, his hat. They even ripped open the linings of his coat. The prisoner stood nearly naked in the road, yet no paper had been found. At length they pulled off his boots. His boots were empty; but they heard the rustle of paper when they were drawn off. The stockings came last, and in his stockings under the soles of his feet were found, in Arnold's handwriting, the treasonable papers, with a plan of the fort, the way to enter it — every

thing, in short, that would make it easy for Clinton to get
possession.

SEARCHING ANDRE.

André was at once taken to the nearest officer and given
up to him as a prisoner. André, true to Arnold even now,

asked that he might be permitted to send a line to him.    As
the papers had not been read, André's request was granted;
and Arnold received a note which told him of André's
arrest.

Of course Arnold knew that his life was now in danger
And so, hurrying from the fort, he leaped a precipice now
called Traitor's Hill, and rode to the nearest boat landing.
Thus he escaped to the British lines, where he put himself
under the protection of Clinton.

The unfortunate André was sentenced to be hanged.
Clinton did all in his power to save the young man, who was
by no means as black-hearted as Arnold; but it was the
army law, and nothing could be done.    Washington tried to
capture Arnold, intending then to release André, and hang
him instead.    The plan failed, however, and André was
doomed to execution.

André wrote a very manly letter to Washington, asking
that he might be shot like a soldier, rather than be hanged
like a dog.    Washington laid this letter before André's
judges, but they would not hear of any other death than
hanging for the unfortunate spy.

"Have you forgotten," said they, "how the British
hanged our brave Nathan Hale — the noble Nathan Hale,
whose last words were, 'I regret that I have but one life to
give for my country' ?  Have you forgotten that they would
not allow him to send one word to his mother, would not

allow him to speak with his old minister?" "No," said they, "André must die as Hale died, — on the gallows."

André met death like a brave man. He hoped to the last that he might be shot and so die a soldier's death; and so when he saw the gallows awaiting him, he gave a start, shuddered, and said, "I am not afraid to die, but I hate this way of dying."

Seeing that all was ready for him, he stepped into the wagon, bandaged his own eyes, fastened the rope about his neck and said, "I pray you to bear me witness that I meet my fate like a brave man." Thus ended Major André's life, a tragedy which is one of the most touching of this whole war.

Arnold, during the remainder of the war, fought on the English side; and at its close, since no one in America had any respect for him, he went to live in England. Even there he was held in contempt by the very ones to whom he had sold himself; so that, since he was a proud man to the end, we know he must have suffered most keenly for his dastardly act.

At one time, while he was living in England, a gentleman who was about to come to America on a visit asked Arnold to give him some letters of introduction to some of the leading families in America. Arnold's reply shows how bitterly he was paying for having sold his own soul. He said, "Alas, in all that great country which gave me birth there is not one man whom I can call friend."

## SURRENDER OF CORNWALLIS.

After the surrender of Burgoyne, there was, I think, never quite such deep despair in the hearts of the Americans.   Still the British were by no means weak.   There were Clinton and Cornwallis with large and powerful armies yet to be defeated.

At last came the final great battle between Cornwallis troops and those of Washington at Yorktown.   Cornwallis had been very busy fortifying this town, into which he had withdrawn his forces.   He had dug trenches, and had thrown up earth works all around the city to keep away Washington's army.   Cornwallis' army had now grown much smaller than the Americans had any idea of.   Indeed he had only 7000 men, 1000 of whom were negro slaves. Washington's army was nearly 16,000, all well trained, and 3000 of them were "picked men" from the Virginia militia.

Clinton had promised, however, to send aid in a week's time surely ; and so Cornwallis felt sure that if he could hold out until then, he should defeat Washington.   On September 28, 1781, the American army marched up and encamped one mile from Yorktown.   Cornwallis withdrew all his forces into the city to wait for Clinton's aid.

The Americans, however, had no thought of waiting.   At once the batteries began their terrible work against the

besieged city.   Gun after gun which the British had placed
upon their walls fell from the hands of the brave Briton
who held it.   The ditches were filled with fragments of the
shattered walls, and heaped with the bodies of the dead
soldiers.

The American forces drew nearer and nearer every night
under cover of the intrenchments which they threw up in
the darkness.  On the evening of the 14th of October,
they had come so close that Washington ordered an imme-
diate attack ; and accordingly two columns were formed —
one French, the other American — to rush upon the city
from the right and from the left.  A hot battle ensued.
Cornwallis, giving up all hope now of aid from Clinton,
and finding himself surrounded on every side, declared all
defence useless, and gave up the struggle.

The general whom Washington appointed to take possession of the defeated army was one who, at a previous battle,
had been defeated by Cornwallis, and had been made to surrender his troops to him.   Cornwallis had at that time been
very severe with the general ; and now he meted out to
Cornwallis the same measure of severity.

The French and American armies were drawn up in two
lines, and between them the conquered army passed.

When they came to stack their arms, the men, most of
them, maintained a sullen silence, shading their faces with
their hats.   Some threw their guns with violence upon the

SURRENDER OF CORNWALLIS AT YORKTOWN.

ground. Some of the officers wept outright at giving up their arms, while others wore a look of haughty defiance, and refused to look upon their conquerors.

Washington and all his officers showed the utmost kindness to their captives. Even Cornwallis, in his report to Clinton, speaks of this, and mentions with great warmth the kindness of the French officers, which he hopes will be remembered in future warfare. But Cornwallis was so deeply humiliated by his conquest that he could hardly appreciate the courtesy of Washington. Once when they were conversing together, Cornwallis stood with his head bare.

"You had better be covered from the cold, my lord," said Washington, politely.

"It does not matter what becomes of this head now," answered Cornwallis, putting his hand to his brow.

With this surrender of Cornwallis, the war was really at an end. The power of the English army was broken. There were battles in other parts of the country after this, but all felt that peace was at hand; and when, at two o'clock in the morning, the news of Washington's great victory reached Philadelphia, the people were awakened by the watchman's cry, "Cornwallis is taken! Cornwallis is taken!"

Lights flashed through the houses, and soon the streets were thronged with crowds eager to learn the glad news.

# Illumination.

COLONEL TILGHMAN, Aid de Camp to his Excellency General WASHINGTON, having brought official acounts of the SURRENDER of Lord Cornwallis, and the Garrifons of York and Gloucefter, thofe Citizens who chufe to ILLUMINATE on the GLORIOUS OCCASION, will do it this evening at Six, and extinguifh their lights at Nine o'clock.

Decorum and harmony are earneftly recommended to every Citizen, and a general difcountenance to the leaft appearance of riot.

*October 24, 1781.*

REDUCED FAC-SIMILE OF THE PROCLAMATION RESPECTING
ILLUMINATION ON THE SURRENDER OF CORNWALLIS.

Some were speechless with delight. Many wept, and the old door-keeper of Congress died of joy. Congress met at an early hour, and that afternoon marched in solemn procession to church to return thanks to God.

As soon as possible, the British army embarked in their vessels, leaving New York once more a free city. Then indeed, there was great rejoicing! There was a great show of fireworks on Bowling Green, where, you remember, had once stood the leaden statue of King George III.

A week later, Washington called together all his officers to bid them farewell, and thank them for their ever ready aid and helpful courage during the terrible war. These brave men who had stood side by side in the bloody battle, facing death together for seven long years, met now together in silence and sadness.

When all were present, Washington raised his glass, and drank to the health of them all. Then he said — and his voice trembled, and there were tears in his eyes, as he spoke, "I cannot come to each of you to take my leave of you; but I shall be glad if each man will come and take me by the hand."

Then General Knox, a man whom Washington loved, came forward, and with tears in his eyes, attempted to speak. Though he could not say one word, Washington understood; and, with tears in his own eyes, drew his friend's head down upon his shoulder and kissed him. Then each

**WASHINGTON TAKING LEAVE OF HIS COMRADES.**

officer came forward to take his leave of his much loved commander; and the bravest men, the most warlike, men who without one tremor had faced the cannon's mouth, men who without a murmur had borne the sufferings of these terrible years, were not ashamed on that day, to let the tears run down their rough sun-burned faces as they said goodby to Washington.

Sometimes I fear we get almost tired of hearing of Washington so much. I confess I often did when I was a child at school. There was the hatchet story of his childhood, the story of his wonderful journey when he was only twenty-one, and the old, old titles of "First President," and "Father of his Country" — yes, I did sometimes say that I was tired of hearing about him; but when I grew older, and I came at last upon a history that told me more about the real character of the man, rather than so much about the battles he fought, and the victories he won, then I came to respect the great heart of the man. He was so brave and daring, and yet always so gentle, so charitable. Although he could dash into the thickest of the fight, yet when the battle was over, and the enemy were taken, you never hear of his blustering about as Burgoyne did, or bullying those who had fallen into his hands as Cornwallis did at the South, or Colonel Prescott at Newport. When a battle was over, he never thought he must celebrate it by getting drunk and making a brute of himself. No, whether in the camp or the drawing-room, whether with friends or with foes, whether conquered or conquering, Washington always thought it worth while to be a gentleman. I do not mean by that an aristocrat — not that; but a real gentleman,— *a gentle man*.

### DATES TO REMEMBER.

Revolution began 1775 — ended 1781. Battle of Lexington April 19, 1775. Battle of Bunker Hill June 17, 1775. Declaration of Independence July 4, 1776.

## Anecdote of Burgoyne.

Nothing, perhaps, helped the colonists on to victory more than the conceit, and consequent unwillingness to learn, of the British generals.

After Bunker Hill, Gen. Gage was, as we know, shut up in the town of Boston by Washington's troops.

As Generals Howe, Clinton, and Burgoyne were sailing up the harbor an outward-bound vessel hailed them, saying, " Your British troops are under seige. Washington's troops surround the city."

" How many are there ? " called Burgoyne.

" Ten thousand colonists to five thousand British."

" What ! " exclaimed Burgoyne puffing himself like a vain frog; " do you mean to say that ten thousand country-clods are keeping under seige ten thousand British troops? Just let us get there and we'll make elbow-room ! "

Boston people did not forget this boast; and a few months later, when Burgoyne and his army were marched as prisoners of war into Cambridge, an old apple-woman, perched with her basket on a fence, made great sport by crying as he passed, " Make way there ! elbow-room ! elbow-room ! "

You remember that it was Burgoyne's troops that used the Old South as a riding-school. Nothing so angered the Boston people as this. And it is said that when, after his surrender, Burgoyne was walking with other generals along Washington Street, he said, as he came to the *Province House*, "There is the former residence of the Governor."

"Yes, shouted a voice in the crowd, "and there opposite is the riding-school."

---

# NANCY HART.

Nancy Hart was known throughout the South in Revolutionary times as "the giantess" and "the heroine of Georgia."

She lived in the wild woods, and supported herself and her children by hunting, fishing, and trapping.

Nancy was not handsome, as she stood over six feet in height, her mop of red hair bundled into a big coil, and her crooked eyes staring and winking as was their custom.

But for all her uncouth appearance, one who knew her said, "Her voice was quiet and soft, and if she had the bravery and courage of a man, she had beneath it all the warm, tender heart of a woman."

She was a fierce supporter of the Whig party from the very outset.

One day six British soldiers, pursuing deserters, came to her cabin for food.

While they were eating, she hid their guns, drove away

their horses, locked her doors, and found a way to send word to her neighbors, "I have trapped six Tories. Come and help me."

During one winter, dressed as a man, she used often to go to the British camp; and, with her sharp, clear perception, she would learn what was going on within, and carry the news to the Whigs.

One day she met a little pale-faced British soldier. Taking his gun from him, she marched him on before her into the Georgian camp.

The Georgian colonel had great confidence in her power and wisdom. So much so, that he once put her in charge of a fort filled with women and children.

Nancy proved, before the colonel's return, that she was equal to the occasion. A company of skirmishers attacked it.

Nancy, in uniform, forced the frightened women to put on their husband's clothes and present themselves upon the walls. She, herself, kept up meanwhile a steady firing from the old cannon.

"I understood the soldiers had gone with Colonel Clarke; but the fort seems only too well manned. We may as well march," said their leader.

When the war was over, a few "squatters," as they were called, came into the country, not far from Nancy's cabin. Nancy fled into the wildernesses of Kentucky. "So many neighbors," said she, "leave me no air to breathe."

## LAFAYETTE.

THE MARQUIS DE LAYFAYETTE.

During this war, the French were our firm allies against the English. One Frenchman, Marquis De Lafayette was so much in sympathy with us, that, nobleman that he was, he left his home and his country to join our army and fight for our cause.

He was young, only nineteen years of age, wealthy, and blessed with everything that should bind his heart to his own home. But so great was his sympathy with the struggling colonies that he was willing to give up all and come to America. "I have always held the cause of America dear," said he; "now I go to serve it personally."

When he arrived, the first act of generosity was to supply clothing and arms to the South Carolina troops, then in great distress.

He wrote at once to Washington saying, "The moment I heard of America I loved her. The moment I heard she was fighting for liberty, I burned with a desire to bleed for her."

Lafayette was so long in this country, and so much heart and soul with us in our fight for independence, that when ever he referred to the Revolution after his return to France, he spoke of himself as an American. One evening, in 1824, while visiting Boston, Mrs. Josiah Quincy said to him:

"The American cockade was black and white, was it not, General?"

"Yes, madam," he replied; "it was black at first, but when the French came and joined *us*, *we* added the white in compliment to them."

At the siege of Yorktown, in the attack which hastened the surrender of Cornwallis, Lafayette and his American division captured one redoubt some minutes before the French carried the redoubt which they commanded.

"You don't remember me, General!" cried an old soldier, pressing through the crowd at the State House to welcome Lafayette on his arrival in Boston. The General looked at him keenly, holding the hand of the old man, who added:

"I was close to you when we stormed our redoubt at Yorktown — I was just behind Captain Smith — you remember Captain Smith? He was shot through the head just as he mounted the redoubt."

"Yes, yes, I remember!" answered Lafayette, his face lightening up. "Poor Captain Smith! *But we beat the French! We beat the French!*"

At the surrender of Cornwallis, the American troops were drawn up on the right, and the French troops on the left of the road, along which the British army marched in solemn silence. Lafayette, noticing that the English soldiers looked only at the Frenchmen on the left, and ignored the American light-infantry, the pride of his heart, and being determined to bring their "eyes to the right," ordered the band to strike up "Yankee Doodle."

"Then," said he, narrating the story, "they did look at us, but were not very well pleased."

——————— *END OF VOLUME I* ———————

## Continue your patriotic journey with

*American History Stories... you never read in school... but should have.*

## Volume II: We the People

Freed from the chains of British tyranny, our forefathers began to construct a new nation. They gathered together the best philosophies and books available and built a republic upon this the American continent. They believed in an incredible truth: that all men were created equal in the eyes of God. They knew their liberty, lives and individuality were rights that could not be denied them by any human government.

In a world accustomed to kings and servants, monarchs and subjects, masters and slaves, these concepts were dangerous and unstoppable. They still are!

Volume II contains the story of the birth of our nation, the signing of the U.S. Constitution, the administrations of such great presidents as George Washington, Thomas Jefferson and James Madison, the War of 1812 and all the struggles that followed. This volume contains more of the history that school books leave out.

Ask for: ISBN 0-9640546-1-2

If you enjoyed these stories of our heritage, you will love the additional stories available for free on our website. Stop by and celebrate our great nation. Isn't it grand to be free! Isn't it grand to be an American!

**Visit http://homepage.mac.com/randallco**

If you would like to receive additional copies of this book for personal, promotional, educational or other reasons, please inquire at your local bookstore or write to:

The Randall Company
P.O. Box 291
Centerville, Utah  84014

Those wishing to obtain a print of "The Prayer At Valley Forge" may call 1-800-4VF-1776 or write to:

Valley Forge Prints
1220 Valley Forge Road
P.O. Box 987/0088
Valley Forge, PA  19482